Pastoral Care
and
Hermeneutics

DONALD CAPPS

Pastoral Care and Hermeneutics

Don S. Browning, *editor*

THEOLOGY AND PASTORAL CARE

FORTRESS PRESS
PHILADELPHIA

Library of Congress Cataloging in Publication Data

Capps, Donald.
   Pastoral care and hermeneutics.

   (Theology and pastoral care series)
   Includes bibliographical references.
    1. Clergy—Office. 2. Hermeneutics. 3. Ricoeur, Paul. 4. Pas-
toral theology. I. Browning, Don S. II. Title. III. Series.
BV660.2.C34 1984   253   84–47909
ISBN 0–8006–1732–0

K956E84   Printed in the United States of America   1–1732

Dedicated to
Edgar Hatfield, Kenneth C. Johnson,
and Karl Redelsheimer

Contents

Series Foreword

Our purpose in the Theology and Pastoral Care Series is to present ministers and church leaders with a series of readable books that will (1) retrieve the theological and ethical foundations of the Judeo-Christian tradition for pastoral care, (2) develop lines of communication between pastoral theology and the other disciplines of theology, (3) create an ecumenical dialogue on pastoral care, and (4) do this in such a way as to affirm, yet go beyond, the recent preoccupation of pastoral care with secular psychotherapy and the other social sciences.

The books in this series are written by authors who are well acquainted with psychology, psychotherapy, and the other social sciences. All of the authors affirm the importance of these disciplines for modern societies and for ministry in particular, but they see them also as potentially destructive of human values unless they are guided in their practical application by tested religious and ethical traditions. But to retrieve the best of the Judeo-Christian tradition for the church's care and counseling is a challenging, intellectual task—a task to which few writers in the area of pastoral care have attended with sufficient thoroughness. This series addresses that task out of a broad ecumenical stance, with all of the authors taking an ecumenical approach to theology. Besides a vigorous investigation of Protestant resources, there are specific treatments of pastoral care in Judaism and Catholicism.

We hope that the series will help ministers and church leaders view afresh the theological and ethical foundations of care and counseling. All of the books have a practical dimension, but even more important than that, they help us see care and counseling differently. Compared with writings of the last thirty years in this field, some of the books will seem startlingly different. They will need to be read and pondered with care. But I have little doubt that the series will make a profound and lasting impact upon the way we understand and practice our care for one another.

In *Pastoral Care and Hermeneutics,* Don Capps has provided a long-awaited bridge between interpretation theory in pastoral care and theology. For several decades theology has depended upon various theories about what it means to interpret a text. In recent years the names of Schleiermacher, Dilthey, Hans-Georg Gadamer, and Paul Ricoeur have dominated discussions about the nature of hermeneutics, and these debates have had enormous influence upon contemporary theology. But the ministry student and minister have often been left in a state of perplexity as to just what all of these important conversations about the nature of interpretation theory or hermeneutics might mean for their praxis as ministers and religious leaders. Now for the first time Don Capps has given us a significant statement relating hermeneutics as it is discussed within the context of theology and biblical studies to the practical theological area of pastoral care.

The work of Paul Ricoeur provides a seminal resource. Capps uses Ricoeur to investigate the question of the similarities between interpreting a classic text such as the Bible and interpreting a meaningful human action as an act of care or the actions of a human in need. Both the text and the human action have a meaning that goes beyond the "ostensive reference" or the meaning intended by the author. They also both give rise to a more objective meaning—a vision of a certain way of being-in-the-world—which goes beyond the original intentions or the original situation of their authors. The task of hermeneutics is to capture this deeper meaning. The process of interpretation is basically the same whether we are interpreting a scripture or a concrete pastoral act in which the minister him- or herself may become involved.

Professor Capps gives us lucid discussions of the role of genre in interpretation and the place of metaphor in the creation of meaning. In the final sections of the book he investigates leading metaphors in pastoral care, such as "shepherd," "wounded healer," and "wise fool," and relates them to various kinds of pastoral acts.

Don Capps has emerged within recent years as one of the leading writers working in that area of practical theology dealing with pastoral care. His *Life Cycle Theory and Pastoral Care,* an earlier contribution to this series, is widely read and appreciated. *Pastoral Care and Hermeneutics* promises not only to enrich concrete pastoral practice but to constitute a major bridge relating the theoretical concerns of contemporary theology to the practical concerns of pastoral care and counseling.

DON S. BROWNING

Introduction

Pastoral actions are occurring all the time. The bereaved are being comforted. The homebound and institutionalized are being visited. The lonely, depressed, and frightened are receiving words of pastoral encouragement. Alcoholics, rape victims, drug abusers, couples planning marriage, and couples contemplating divorce are being counseled. Such pastoral acts are so common as to be almost routine. Yet they are anything but routine. Each is unique unto itself. There is no "textbook" model for any of these actions because in each case there are different persons involved with circumstances and expectations uniquely theirs.

This book is concerned with such pastoral actions. It takes seriously the uniqueness of every pastoral action. Yet it recognizes our need for methods of a more general nature for helping us to understand what effect these actions are having on the lives of the individuals they touch. This book assumes that very few pastors would remain in the ministry if they did not perceive that their actions were having an effect, and that this effect was more often than not gratifying. But this book also assumes that we do not have very good methods at the present time for understanding what really takes place in such pastoral actions. Nor do we have very good methods for evaluating the effects of such actions once we have a fairly good understanding of them.

The premise of this book is that hermeneutics, or the science of interpretation, is a very promising method available to us today for understanding and evaluating pastoral actions. This is certainly not an original idea with me. A number of persons have recommended this pastoral use of hermeneutics in recent publications.[1] Moreover, the seed for this approach was planted years ago through the action-reflection model employed in clinical pastoral education. This model is based on the concept that effective ministry involves the capacity to "reflect" on one's pastoral "actions." Through constructive and nondefensive reflection on selected pastoral acts (often presented in verbatim form), pastors acquire new insights into how they function in the pastoral role.

I have great appreciation for the action-reflection model. But in recent years it has become evident that this model needs refurbishing. It is not explicit enough about what constitutes a pastoral action. Even more important, it is not very clear as to what is involved in "reflecting" on one's pastoral actions. Users of this method explain that "reflection" may involve a number of objective resources as well as subjective insights, including theological and ethical concepts, psychological and sociological theories, and the like. But there has not been much systematic discussion of what each of these resources is expected to contribute to the reflection process. Also, not much attention has been given to what constitutes a reasonably complete reflection on a given action. How do we know when we have reflected enough? How do we know when we have gained true insight into a given pastoral action?

Technically, hermeneutics is concerned with interpretation of texts. Yet, in recent years, the principles of hermeneutics have been applied to phenomena other than texts, and there have been proposals for applying hermeneutics to the sphere of human action. The idea that certain human actions are like texts has caught on, and it has already been applied with notable success to social and political action. There is every reason to believe that this idea will be equally useful for interpreting pastoral actions such as those that fall under the general heading of pastoral care.

As the table of contents indicates, Paul Ricoeur's hermeneutical theory is fundamental to the approach of this book. I use this theory not only because it is one that I find congenial for the most part, but also it is the theory that is likely to be most accessible to readers of this book. Future books on pastoral hermeneutics are likely to take up other hermeneutical theories, some of which may be critical of Ricoeur. But given the current popularity of Ricoeur's theory, this is a good place for us to begin. Chapter 1 focuses on those features of his hermeneutical theory that are most relevant to the proposed link between texts and action. Chapter 2 then develops a hermeneutical model of *pastoral* action based on Ricoeur's theory. It takes up Ricoeur's view that texts and meaningful actions have similar characteristics and applies these characteristics to pastoral actions. Chapters 3–5 take up specific aspects of the hermeneutical model developed in chapter 2, with chapter 3 centering on the important role played by conceptual schemata in interpreting pastoral actions, chapter 4 illustrating a conceptual schema by means of a case study, and chapter 5 exploring how hermeneutics' emphasis on the disclosive effects of pastoral action provides a basis for evaluating such actions.

This book is dedicated to three pastors, Edgar Hatfield, Kenneth C. Johnson, and Karl Redelsheimer. Among the many parish pastors I have known through the years, these three have taught me the most about ministry. In chapter 3 I discuss three pastoral models (shepherd, wounded healer, and wise fool),[2] and in chapter 5 I link them to three types of Christian self-understanding (the responsible self, believable self, and accessible self). These three pastors have reflected all three dimensions of Christian ministry and self-understanding, but each has also communicated to me and to others the unique strengths and potentialities of one of these dimensions. Thus individually and collectively, their pastoral careers and exemplification of the Christian life have been a testimony to me and others of the fullness of the Christian experience.

I especially want to thank James Hulsey for providing me the case study introduced in chapter 4. I am also indebted to Gene Fowler, a doctoral candidate in pastoral theology at Princeton Theological Seminary, whose own scholarly and pastoral interests directly parallel the topics and themes of this book. I have profited immensely from conversations with him, especially his insights into the role of the self in the hermeneutical process. I also want to thank my wife, Karen, and son, John, for their support of me in what I like to believe is one of the more harmless addictions seminary professors are prone to, the writing of books. I trace this addiction to my father's example. His newsletters to our local church's military personnel serving in World War II are undoubtedly the prototype for my own efforts to write to and for pastors who are also on the firing line.

CHAPTER 1

Ricoeur's Theory of Hermeneutics

What is hermeneutics? According to Norman Perrin, hermeneutics is "the methodology for reaching an understanding of written texts held to be meaningful."[1] By emphasizing that hermeneutics is a methodology, Perrin and others engaged in hermeneutics oppose the idea that interpretation of texts is an exclusively intuitive act. Understanding a text requires the use of methods and principles of interpretation. As a science of interpretation with a long history, hermeneutics' traditional emphasis has been the development of principles and methods for interpreting written texts, particularly the Bible and other classical texts. In recent decades other forms of expression have come under its purview, including music, film, painting, and sculpture. Still, it is safe to say that the written text remains the primary focus of hermeneutics, and that the inclusion of other art forms within the study of hermeneutics is based largely on the fact that they have certain resemblances to texts.

Following Friedrich Schleiermacher, who has been called the father of modern hermeneutics, a major goal of those engaged in hermeneutics has been to develop a general science of interpretation, one whose principles and methods would be applicable to all written texts held to be meaningful. For Schleiermacher and his successors, hermeneutics would be a science that cut across scholarly disciplines, having value for any and every discipline involving the interpretation of texts. This goal implied that all texts were to be treated alike in that all would be approached with clearly formulated principles and methods. The Bible or other sacred texts would not be treated differently in principle from texts for which divine authorship was not at issue. This did not mean that all texts would be interpreted by the very same methods. A general science of hermeneutics would need to take seriously the fact that texts belong to various genres, and some methods appropriate to one genre may not be appropriate to another. But it was hoped that it would be possible to establish certain methodological principles that apply to interpretation of all texts.

While this hope has not been realized, hermeneuticians have made considerable progress in identifying the major issues involved in developing a methodology for interpreting a given text. In the following discussion, I will identify a number of these issues, centering on Paul Ricoeur's approach to them.[2]

THE AUTHOR'S INTENTION

A fundamental issue for interpretation of a text is the question: How important are the author's intentions for understanding the meaning of a text? Some hermeneuticians have argued that to interpret a text adequately we need to know what the author was consciously striving to achieve. Those who take this view will try to find out as much as they can about the author's composition of the text. They want to know what was happening in the author's life at the time the book was written. They want to know what the author was thinking and feeling, and especially what the author meant, purposefully, to communicate. To discover this, they often comb through the author's letters and journals to find out what the author intended to accomplish in the text.

But other hermeneuticians, Ricoeur among them, say that we should not pay too much attention to what was going on in the life and mind of the author when the text was being written. They say that the author's intentions should have relatively little to do with the interpretation of the text. The text stands on its own. It is an objective reality to which all interpreters now have access, whereas the intentions of the author are a very subjective matter which even the author, now that the text is written, may not be very clear about. To make the interpretation dependent on recapturing the author's conscious intentions places hermeneutics on a very unstable footing.

Critics of this view may cite instances where the meaning of a given text was impossible to decipher without crucial inside information about the author's intentions. For example, a writer may have politically dangerous things to say and thus resort to allegory to communicate his views. It may be necessary for the reader to know the identities of the persons being allegorized in order to understand what the text means. If the reader lacks such knowledge, so the argument goes, the author's intentions and hence the whole meaning of the text are inaccessible to the reader. But Ricoeur points out that texts have multiple meanings. It may be that one level of meaning will be accessible only to those who possess such inside information. But this would only apply to what he calls the *ostensive referential meaning* of the text, that is, the local or immediate situation to which it is addressed. This ostensive level of meaning may have little to do with its other referential meanings which, in the long run, may be more significant. Texts rarely survive on the basis of their ostensive meaning alone. Biblical texts, for example, do not become meaningless to us simply because their ostensive meanings may be inaccessible or matters for conjecture. Conversely, the meaning of a text has not been exhausted when we have ascertained its ostensive references. Thus Ricoeur downplays the author's intentions in the interpretation of texts. He believes we should focus our attention on the text itself, which is available to us as an objective reality, and not on the mind of the author, which is no longer accessible.

THE STATUS OF THE READER

Another important issue for interpretation of a text is the question, Does any given reader have privileged status with regard to understanding a given text? Especially, are the readers for whom the text was originally intended in a better position to understand it than those who are not part of the original readership? This question is important for hermeneutics because most texts are read not only by those for whom they were originally written but also by various others for whom the text was not explicitly written. True, some texts are destroyed as soon as they have served the purposes of their immediate audience. Grocery lists are like this. So are TV guides. Other texts survive the immediate occasion for which they were written, but only because those for whom they were originally written have reason to believe they may need to refer to them later. Business letters and committee reports are examples of such texts. However, most texts not only survive the immediate occasion for which they were written but also fall into the hands of readers for whom they were not originally intended. The obvious example is classic literature (the Bible, Shakespeare) that has survived for many generations and has been read by publics hardly envisioned by the original authors. The question is, Do the original readers have a privileged status with regard to interpretation of such texts? Does the community to whom the Gospel of Mark was originally written have privileged access to this text such that all subsequent interpreters are inevitably in a secondary position with respect to understanding its meaning? Or is the reverse actually the case? Are readers who are less caught up in the immediacy of the original context in a privileged position to understand the text because they are able to view it in light of subsequent human experience? This issue arises because texts, unlike spoken discourse, transcend local contexts, both spatially and temporally.

Ricoeur's answer to this question can be anticipated from our comments on the referential meanings of a text. Basically, he does not believe that the original audience to which a text was addressed has a privileged status *with respect to the text*. They may of course be persons with privileged status on other grounds, such as the fact that the original audience for Mark's Gospel was closer in time to the Christ event, and thus have privileged status on personal, social, or historical grounds. But Ricoeur argues that they have no privileged status with respect to the text itself because all readers, no matter who they are, are in the position of having to interpret the text. There is an inevitable distance between reader and text, and this is even true for the author who, having written the text, is now in the position of being a reader of it. The real issue for Ricoeur is not whether some readers have immediate access to the text and others do not but the effect of the inevitable distance between reader and text. How is this distance bridged? How does this distance affect the reader's understanding of the text? Is greater distance from the text a positive or negative factor in understanding it? I will return to Ricoeur's views on this distance issue later. In the meantime, we can readily see that the issue of the status of the reader is part of a much larger issue, the relation between reader and text.

THE RELATION BETWEEN
READER AND TEXT

What is the relation between the reader and the text? What happens when a reader encounters the text? The basic answer that hermeneutics gives is this: The reader engages in the act of *understanding* the text. The object is not to count the number of words on the page, admire the typescript, or even memorize the text. It is, first and foremost, to *understand the meaning of the text*. There are two very critical issues here. First, early in the development of hermeneutics as a general science, it was recognized that the act of understanding what a text means has a certain circularity about it. That is, we are only able to grasp the meaning of a text if we are already able in some sense to understand it. In a sense, grasping its meaning depends on a certain preunderstanding that is only accessible through the text itself. For those who are faced with a particularly difficult text, the circularity of the interpretive act appears very much like a Catch-22 situation.

Ricoeur accepts the fact that understanding a text is circular, and he resists the idea that we can somehow break out of this circle. But he believes that hermeneutics can be very useful in preventing the task of understanding a text from becoming a vicious circle. Later in this chapter I will discuss in some detail his own carefully formulated proposal for reducing the viciousness of the hermeneutical circle.

A second and related issue is the question, What in fact is the object of interpretation? Is it the text? This seems obvious. Might it also be the reader? This seems less obvious, but for Ricoeur it is a very important aspect of the reader-text relationship. We know of course that the reader is involved in grasping the meaning of the text. But Ricoeur also points out that the interpretive process is reciprocal, that in a very real sense the text interprets the reader. Take, for example, the experience of finding a parking citation on the windshield of one's car. As one reads the citation, one attempts to grasp the meaning of this text. How much will it cost? How close was I to getting back before the ticket was issued? Should I conceal the fact that I received the ticket from my parents, my spouse, my children? But the parking citation also interprets the reader. It evokes a variety of responses which interpret us, telling us something about ourselves that in this instance we are likely not to want to have revealed to us. It may disclose our low threshold for frustration and anger, our capacity to conceive petty acts of revenge or rebellion when frustrated and angry, and our ability to lay the blame for our negligent behavior on any number of scapegoats.

What enables a text to interpret the reader? It is not that the text is actually about the reader. This only happens when we read a biography about ourselves or autobiography written by ourselves. Rather, it is that the text, as Ricoeur puts it, "discloses a world" which we as readers appropriate. Admittedly, the parking citation is not an impressive kind of text. But like all meaningful texts it discloses a world to its reader, a "world" that condemns the reader (by charging the reader with a specific offense of negligence), offers terms for restitution (a stated fine) or further recourse (a court date if the reader wishes to protest innocence), and a threat of further consequences if the fine is not paid by a specified date. The world disclosed is one in which the reader must make restitution or establish innocence of the offense; there is no other avenue of escape. Note that the citation says nothing specifically about the reader. Yet it interprets the reader through condemnation, offer of opportunities for restitution, and so forth. The only way the reader can resist this interpretation is to refuse to appropriate the world disclosed in the text by declining to enter that world.

This is where the issue of different sets of readers and their status regarding the text comes back into play. We may assume that the reader for whom the citation was originally written has very little opportunity to refuse to appropriate the world disclosed in the text. But passersby who see the parking citation on the windshield may also appropriate this text. They may view this text with a sense of relief ("I'm glad it wasn't me"), but they too are being interpreted by it ("this could happen to you"). The only readers who could be justified in refusing to appropriate the text are those who never park automobiles in metered spaces, and yet they too may find themselves being interpreted by this text if it calls to mind other situations of personal negligence ("I forgot to replace the furnace filter last month").

Thus for Ricoeur the relationship between reader and text is one of reciprocal interpretation. We interpret texts but texts also interpret us. How do texts do this? For Ricoeur a text's power to interpret us is due to its capacity to disclose possible "worlds" to which we may orient ourselves. These worlds are not limited to the ostensive referential meaning of a text. In fact, Ricoeur argues that the world-disclosive power of a text is due precisely to the fact that the text is not limited to its ostensive meaning: 'For us, the world is the ensemble of references *opened up* by the text," that is, its "nonsituational references." He continues:

> Thus we speak about the "world" of Greece, not to designate any more what were the situations for those who lived then, but to designate the non-situational references which outlive the effacement of the first and which henceforth are offered as possible modes of being, as symbolic dimensions of our being-in-the-world.[3]

He concludes that "for me, this is the referent of all literature; no longer the *Umwelt* of the ostensive references of dialogue, but the *Welt* projected by the nonostensive references of every text that we have read, understood, and loved."[4] The world of a text is the meanings it opens up or discloses beyond the limits of its situational meanings.

But how does this world interpret us? What is the reader's relationship to this world? Ricoeur says that to "understand a text is at the same time to light up our own situation, or, if you will, to interpolate among the predicates of our situation all the significations which make a *Welt* of our *Umwelt*."[5] Thus the text interprets us by lighting up our own situation and "enlarging" it into a world. Then we are no longer confined by the limits of *our* situation but oriented to the world that has been opened up for us. The text has thereby freed us "from the visibility and limitation of situations by opening up a world for us, that is, new dimensions of our being-in-the-world."[6] Thus the relationship of reader to text is not merely one in which the situation of the text speaks to the situation of the reader. Rather the text opens a world that transcends the situation of the text. It is this world that addresses the situation of the reader. When it does so, it enlarges the reader's situation into a world that also transcends his or her own immediate situation.

I will return throughout this book to Ricoeur's view that texts interpret readers through their world-disclosive power. This way of understanding the effect of texts on readers is directly relevant to pastoral care. If texts enable readers to see beyond the limits of their situation and to orient themselves to an enlarged world, then texts may serve as models for pastoral work whose purpose is also to help persons see beyond the limits of their situation. Later, I will discuss in more detail Ricoeur's own application of this view of texts to the world of human action.

THE ROLE OF GENRE

Another important issue for hermeneutics is the role of genre in the interpretation of texts. Much of Ricoeur's own work is concerned with developing general hermeneutical principles irrespective of genre consideration. But as his work in biblical hermeneutics clearly demonstrates, he has also given considerable attention to the hermeneutics of specific genres. In his view, genre issues impinge directly on the relation between reader and text. This is because the genre of a text has considerable influence on the nature of the world disclosed by the text. For example, the genre of the epic (whether classical tales involving the exploits of Odysseus and El Cid, or more contemporary examples like Ole Edvart Rolvaag's account of the fate of Norwegian immigrants in *Giants of the Earth*) discloses a world in which individuals of extraordinary courage, deep vision, uncommon virtue, and passion for ideals struggle against powerful forces that put their commitment to the ultimate test. The parable form is also about people meeting challenges, but the emphasis is very different. Here, individuals are not confronted by powerful forces which threaten their moral resolve, but by deceptively ordinary events that prove to be quite extraordinary inasmuch as they upset a person's normal perceptions of reality and challenge one to see the world in an entirely new way. The world disclosed by the parable form is not one in which one is confronted by a powerful force, but by an ambiguous situation in which one is hard pressed to know how to react.

Since genres are an important factor in texts' disclosures of worlds, it is very useful to compare genres in terms of the world-disclosures they make possible. In some cases, two genres may disclose worlds that, while different, are yet compatible to one another. In other cases, two genres may treat us to a clash of worlds. Often a particular genre was developed precisely to confront another popular genre with a new and radically different disclosure. Thus there is value in the hermeneutician becoming familiar with the properties of various literary genres, because the genre is an important determinant of the world disclosed in a text.

One of Ricoeur's most interesting discussions of the genre issue is his essay "Toward a Hermeneutic of the Idea of Revelation."[7] Here he discusses five genres of biblical literature, which he calls prophetic, narrative, prescriptive, wisdom, and hymnic discourse. His primary concern is to explore the theological idea of revelation through hermeneutics, which in this case means focusing on the "modalities of discourse" that are most formative of a community of faith. He shows how each of these five genres is concerned with the revelation of God, but each conceives revelation in a different way. Prophetic discourse conceives revelation as the speech of God behind the speech of the prophet; revelation is understood as a "double voice." Narrative discourse conceives a founding event such as the exodus as the imprint of God's act; God was revealed in this event of history, and the revelation is kept alive and current through recitation of the story of this event. Prescriptive discourse is revelation in the form of instruction, but instruction organically connected to the founding event preserved in narrative discourse. Wisdom discourse addresses the individual and through the individual every human being; its themes are human limit situations such as solitude, suffering, fault, and death: "What is revealed is the possibility of hope in spite of. . . ."[8] Hymnic discourse is revelatory through its formation of emotions that transcend the everyday situations that inspire them; where wisdom discourse centers on the discouraging limit situations of life, hymnic discourse typically involves thanksgiving, praise, and anticipatory supplication.

As Ricoeur points out, these literary genres are the very forms in which revelation is expressed. These forms are not tangential to the revelation. Also, the interplay between these forms communicates the community's experience of God's revelation. Some genres are mutually supportive as, for example, the fact that prescriptive discourse and narrative discourse both locate revelation in the founding event. Others focus on contrasting dimensions of God's revelation, as in wisdom and hymnic discourse. Ricoeur concludes that since the forms or genres of religious discourse are so important, revelation is not univocal (meaning of "one voice") but polysemic, or consisting of various meanings. Also, as the history of any community of faith attests, revelation always has the potential for appearing in new forms.

Ricoeur's analysis of biblical genres points up the importance of the genre for determining the text's world-disclosures. On the one hand, only certain kinds of written discourse are able to disclose the world of God's revelation, and these biblical forms are therefore special in that regard. On the other hand, these biblical forms reflect a trait of all literary forms, namely, that the form determines what kinds of world-disclosures are possible for a text written in that particular form.

This may not appear to be an issue of great importance for pastoral care until we apply it to Ricoeur's proposed analogy between texts and human actions. I will discuss this analogy in much greater detail later, but we can note here that human actions are like texts in the sense that they too take different forms. This is certainly true for pastoral care actions. Premarital counseling and grief counseling are uniquely different forms or genres of pastoral care. Thus we would expect that they would make possible different sorts of world-disclosures. Furthermore, as I suggested in *Biblical Approaches to Pastoral Counseling*, there may be a more direct relationship between biblical forms and forms of pastoral care, such that the psalm form relates to grief counseling, the proverb form to premarital counseling, and the parable form to marriage counseling.[9] The

rationale for relating certain biblical genres to certain forms of
pastoral action is that they envision similar world-disclosures which,
in this case, means similar understandings of how God is revealed in
human situations.

However, genre is only one of two important elements in the text's
capacity for world-disclosure. The second to which we now turn our
attention is the very important matter of metaphor.

THE ROLE OF METAPHOR

We have discussed Ricoeur's emphasis on the power of a text to
break through the limitations of its immediate situation and to
disclose a world. The question this obviously raises is this: How does
the text do this? The genre may determine what kinds of world-
disclosures are possible in a given text, but what is it that actually
effects the world-disclosure? Ricoeur's general answer to this question is that language has multiple meanings (it is polysemic). Thus, a
text may have meaning in relation to the immediate situation and at
the same time mean something more than this. It is this polysemic
characteristic of language that enables it to have ostensive meaning
(Umwelt) and meanings that disclose a world *(Welt).* Ricoeur points
out that there is a form of language that does on a smaller scale what
meaningful texts do on the larger scale. This is the metaphor.
Metaphors have the same dual characteristics as meaningful texts in
that they too make ostensive references and disclose worlds. In fact,
in metaphorical language, the ostensive reference is the springboard
for the world-disclosure. The world-disclosure occurs when the
metaphorical idea is freed from its ostensive meaning, but without
this ostensive meaning, there would be no world-disclosure.

Take, for example, the biblical proverb, "A person without self-
control is like a city broken into and left without walls" (Prov. 25:28).
This is a metaphorical statement. Its ostensive reference is the city
that has been broken into and left without walls, a situation well
known to the original readers of this proverb. Its world-disclosure
emerges from its proposal that a man without self-control is like such
a city. Through this metaphor, the proverb provides a new understanding of what it means to lack self-control.

This may seem a rather modest world-disclosure, but it is a disclosure nonetheless. The world of the loss of self-control has been
opened up for us by viewing it through the image of a city without
walls. Once it is opened up for us in this fashion, we might wish to go
on to specify its meanings more precisely, or put more explicitly

what the metaphor leaves suggestive. We might say that persons without self-control are more susceptible to various destructive influences from without, and then go on to specify what these destructive influences might be. In this way the metaphor gives rise to concepts that may eventually be developed into models or schemata of thought. If we wanted to we could probably develop this line of thinking into a rather sophisticated theory of self-control.

Ultimately, then, the ability of a metaphor to disclose a world is in its capacity to stimulate a thought process that results in the development of conceptual models, schemata, or theories. A single metaphor may not be able to carry this conceptual process alone. But a loose collection of metaphors may do so. The metaphor we have just used to illustrate how metaphorical language is world-disclosive is one of a number of metaphors in the Book of Proverbs that draw an analogy between human society (the city) and the individual (a man without self-control). Other proverbs draw a similar analogy between the natural world and the individual: "Like clouds and wind without rain is a person who boasts of a gift he does not give" (Prov. 25:14). These metaphors when collected together in the Book of Proverbs begin to create a model of human life in which these three social, natural, and personal spheres comprise an all-embracing order to life. In turn, this model implies that God is revealed through this all-embracing order.[10] When metaphorical thinking gives rise to the concept of an all-embracing order to life, then it has created a model by which much of what happens in the world of human action can be understood. Unlike the single metaphor, the model provides a basic orientation to life for those who are disposed to appropriate it.

In short, essentially the same process involved in understanding the meaning of a metaphor is involved in understanding the world-disclosure of a text. There is the same movement from the ostensive referential meaning of the text to its world-disclosive meanings. Also, as with the metaphor, when these world-disclosive meanings have been appropriated by the reader, we say that the reader has understood the text and the text has interpreted the reader.

THE LANGUAGE SYSTEM

Understanding the text through personal appropriation of its world-disclosive meanings is one essential aspect of the interpretation of a text. But for Ricoeur there is another equally essential aspect of the hermeneutical process. This is the task of *explaining* the text's world-disclosive power. In Ricoeur's view, the act of understanding a text is "subjective" in the sense that it results in a personal appropriation of the text. But interpretation of a text must also be "objective" if the hermeneutical process is not to become a *vicious* circle. This is where explanation of how the text works comes into play. Without it, the process of understanding a text does not escape the pure subjectivity of the reader. Ricoeur says that we are not doomed to this vicious circle if we bring a concern for explanation into the hermeneutical process. For him, this entails analysis of the language system of the text, an analysis that identifies the "logic" of its language structure before any interpretation of the meaning of the text is attempted.

To illustrate how this structural analysis works, Ricoeur cites Claude Lévi-Strauss's analyses of the structure of myths, which show that myths typically consist of a whole system of oppositions and combinations (birth-death, light-darkness, good-evil, and so forth). When we focus on the language structure and not the specific meaning of the text, we are engaged in an exercise of explanation that is integral to understanding the text. It is designed to put the process of understanding on an objective footing. It is true that analysis of the structure of the text cannot be done in a purely objective manner. But this does not concern Ricoeur because his goal is not pure objectivity, even in the explanatory aspect of the process, but a personal appropriation of the text that is chastened or purified by taking the objectivity of the text seriously. And this is best done through analysis of the structure of the text, because such analysis is not yet concerned with discernment of its meanings. The question of the meaning of the text is temporarily postponed so that when this question is raised, it will be informed by analysis of the text's language system.

Ricoeur's own analysis of the structure of metaphorical language provides a useful illustration of how such analysis informs one's understanding of the text. For him, the analogical structure of metaphorical language does two things. It establishes a similarity between two phenomena (city without walls—person without self-control), but it also acknowledges their dissimilarity. A city is not identical to a person nor is a person identical to a city. Thus, structural analysis of metaphorical language clarifies its language structure in terms of an opposition involving similarity and dissimilarity. This analysis in turn influences Ricoeur's understanding of the meaning of any given metaphor. Viewing Jesus' parables as metaphors ("the kingdom of God is like a man who discovered a treasure in a field"), he emphasizes the similarity between the two phenomena (the kingdom of God does resemble the discovery of a hidden treasure) but also the implied dissimilarity. The kingdom of God is not identical to the discovery of a hidden treasure. It is potentially more life shattering. If winning the state lottery causes many people to quit their jobs and buy new homes, the kingdom of God is like this and more: "The kingdom of God is like a man who won a million dollars in a state lottery. When he refused to claim his prize, his relatives rose up to kill him." Or, "The kingdom of God is like a woman who won a million dollars in the state lottery and immediately left her husband and children."

Often, Ricoeur's own interpretation of a metaphor will emphasize the world-disclosing power of the dissimilarity, once the similarity has been affirmed. Sallie McFague uses Luther's mediating position between the Catholic and Zwinglian view of the Eucharist to illustrate this point:

> To Luther, the bread and wine were still symbols of Christ's body and blood, still participated in that reality, but in a way that I would call "metaphorical," for the assertions "This is my body" and "This is my blood" were not viewed as identity statements, but as including a silent but present negative. One critical difference between symbolic and metaphorical statements is that the latter always contain the whisper, "it is *and it is not*."[11]

This example illustrates how dissimilarity, once similarity has been established, is a vitally important factor in the world-disclosing power of metaphor. The dissimilarity introduces ambiguity and paradox into the process of understanding.

Or consider Robert Frost's famous poem "The Road Not Taken." On one level this poem can be understood as a person walking in the woods—simply that. But then as the poem develops we sense that it is about something more momentous. "Somewhere ages and ages hence" and "that has made all the difference" are lines that suggest the walk in the woods is a metaphor for the journey of life. Thus something known (a fork in the road) becomes disclosive of something less understandable: how it is that our lives occasionally involve decisions where choosing one alternative means rejecting another. As far as we can tell, either alternative would have been worthy, almost equally so, of our pursuit or commitment. This similarity between a fork in the road and confronting a life decision is certainly part of the disclosiveness of the poem. But once this similarity has been established, what is more disclosive is the dissimilarity between the walk in the woods and the journey of life. As the poem develops, it reveals a truth about the course of human life that is not as true of walking in the woods. In human life, it is unlikely that once we have made the decision, we will later take up the alternative originally passed over. Frost's observation that "knowing how way leads on to way, I doubted if I should ever come back" is far more true of the course of life than of walking in the woods. Thus the metaphor also reveals a significant dissimilarity between the known (walk in woods) and lesser known (journey of life), and this difference is also part of what enables the metaphor to disclose a world. This is also a more disturbing disclosure, because it suggests that in human life the desire to double back and make a different start is rarely realized.

Thus, structural analysis of the language system of metaphor is vitally important to our understanding of metaphor. Without it, we risk collapsing the distance between human situations (a man who finds a buried treasure) and the sphere of God's activity (kingdom of God).

THE MEANING SYSTEM

This analysis of metaphorical language is an example of what Ricoeur means by structural analysis of a text's language system. Ricoeur is careful to emphasize that structural analysis of this sort cannot take the place of interpretation of a text's system of meanings. It is only an aid toward interpretation. But we should also note that when Ricoeur addresses the meanings of a text, his interpretation remains quite analytical. The movement from explanation to understanding means leaving the structural analysis of language behind, but what replaces it is not an intuitive reading of the text where we are free to decide on purely arbitrary grounds how we choose to read it. Rather, Ricoeur takes the view that a text's meanings are communicated through structures of thought, and these are crucial to understanding the world disclosed by the text.

Take, for example, Ricoeur's view that the parables of Jesus exhibit a pattern of orientation, disorientation, and reorientation. As McFague describes this view: "A parable begins in the ordinary world with its conventional standards and expectations, but in the course of the story a radically different perspective is introduced that disorients the listener, and finally, through the interaction of the two competing viewpoints, tension is created that results in a redescription of life in the world."[12] Ricoeur says that this pattern is reflected in the parables as a whole, and that "we have to grasp them as a whole and to understand each one in the light of the other. The Parables make sense together."[13] Ricoeur recognizes that discovery of this pattern is a disappointment to some because it implies that the tension is never overcome, that the parables do not go beyond metaphorical thinking to a coherent theological idea that resolves this tension: "At the very moment that they call for theological clarification, they start shattering the theological simplifications which we attempt to put in their place."[14] But this disappointment may be replaced by amazement when we begin to appreciate that the power of metaphorical language is precisely "that it abides to the end *within* the tension created by the images" and that "there is more to *think through* the richness of the images than in the coherence of a simple concept."[15] The parables do not give us "any conceptual system about God and his action among us." But what they do give us is a structure of thought based on this pattern of orientation, dis-orientation, and reorientation.

This example illustrates how, for Ricoeur, understanding the meanings of a text begins with the meaning system. If a similarity-dissimilarity structure characterizes the parables' metaphorical language system, an orientation-disorientation-reorientation pattern characterizes their system of meaning. Ricoeur sees this pattern as evidence or even proof of the text's disclosive power. In the case of Jesus' parables, it is the metaphorical language that *enables* them to be world-disclosive. But only by identifying the inner structure of their meaning system are we able to explain how they effect such world-disclosure. The parables disclose a world by effecting a dis-orientation from the conventional viewpoint to which they initially orient the reader, and then sustaining an unresolvable tension be-tween these two conflicting viewpoints.

I will return to this issue when I take up Ricoeur's view that understanding human action is similar in principle to understand-ing a text. As with texts, Ricoeur argues that human actions have systems of meaning. Thus, understanding a given human action involves identifying the meaning system's inner structure. Ricoeur recommends the use of theories and conceptual schemata for analyzing the meaning systems of human actions because their struc-tures are seldom self-evident. For human actions, the major source of such theories is the social sciences, but because hermeneutics aims at being a general science, the humanities are also an important source of theories and conceptual schemata. (The converse is also true for the study of texts. Social-scientific theories and concepts originally designed for the study of human action may also be applicable to texts.)

THE PROBLEM OF
CRITICAL DISTANCE

A problem that is directly related to the preceding discussion of how we gain understanding of the text's meanings is the issue of critical distance in understanding a text. As we have seen, Ricoeur contends that the hermeneutical circle becomes vicious if there are no objective and explanatory procedures in the hermeneutical process. Without these it is essentially intuitive and thus becomes a vicious circle because it traps us as readers in our own subjectivity.

We have already discussed some of the procedures that the reader may use to overcome the viciousness of this circle. One is to engage in structural analysis of the language system of the text. Another is to identify the structure of the text's system of meanings. Both procedures place the task of understanding the text on a more objective footing. Even though the end result of the hermeneutical process is our personal appropriation of the text (through orienting ourselves to its world-disclosures), the path to this personal appropriation has been cleared away by these more objective procedures.

In Ricoeur's judgment, however, this achievement of greater objectivity is bought at a price. Through these procedures we approach the text with a critical distance. Where previously we would have read the text with a certain intuitive naiveté, we now approach it as a text held somewhat at arm's length. On the other hand, Ricoeur defends the use of such procedures to "objectify" the text if they enable the text to speak for itself, and thus assist it in becoming world-disclosive.

Another form of critical distance, however, is potentially far more damaging to the reader's relationship to the text. This is what Ricoeur calls the "hermeneutics of suspicion." Supposing, says Ricoeur, that we have been the victim of a ruse where, having received a letter, we discover that it was not sent by the person we believed to have sent it. The problem here is not the content of the letter—its meanings—but its origins. The letter did not come from where we thought. This deception creates suspicion regarding the origin of the letter, which in turn prompts us to interpret the letter not for its actual content but for its false origins.[16]

Ricoeur points out that Marx, Nietzsche, and Freud ushered in a new era of hermeneutical work, the era of hermeneutical suspicion. For them, a major function of hermeneutics is to show that the texts they were concerned with had their origins in a "false consciousness." That is, the texts originated from an illusory view of reality. This was not attributable to any false or deceptive intention of the authors, but to the fact that the texts reflected an illusion deeply rooted in the culture. Thus Marx, Nietzsche, and Freud's suspicion was directed to the cultural convictions and values that gave rise to the texts. Nor, in the final analysis, was their suspicion directed only to written texts, because in Ricoeur's judgment, all three viewed culture as itself a text and each employed himself in exposing the illusions behind this text. They saw no merit in trying to understand and appropriate the culture's world-disclosures because they were convinced that these had their origin in a false consciousness. For Marx it was the false consciousness of domination and submission, for Nietzsche of will, and for Freud of desire.

Ricoeur calls this exposure of false consciousness an act of *demystification*. It differs from *demythologization*. In demythologization, the reader views the text as one of true consciousness in its essential meanings but recognizes that the text contains material attributable to the cultural mythology, and judges this material to be an impediment for the modern reader to appropriate the world-disclosive meanings of the text. Furthermore, demythologization is concerned that the world-disclosive meanings of a text may themselves become assimilated to another culture's natural cognitive systems and thus lose their world-disclosive power. Ricoeur points out that this is what happened to the Old Testament during the New Testament era, and that this is what may well be happening to the New Testament in our own era. The hermeneutical problem that demythologization addresses is what to do so that the New Testament will not become a second Old Testament. Demystification thus differs from demythologization in that the former considers the text to be fundamentally the product of false consciousness whereas the latter conceives it to be fundamentally true but containing elements that must be cleared away so that the text is not misconstrued as the product of false consciousness.

We cannot discuss Ricoeur's analysis of these three demystification projects (Marx, Nietzsche, Freud) in any detail. But we need to note that, in his view, none of these critiques of false consciousness was intended as an end in itself. It was the means toward new affirmations. The hermeneutics of suspicion uncovers the false consciousness of a text not in the interests of destroying but for the purpose of recovering true consciousness. Or, as Ricoeur puts it, "Destruction . . . is a moment in every new foundation. The 'destruction' of hidden worlds is a positive task."[17] The affirmation that Ricoeur attributes to Marx is perhaps the most significant for our purposes here because it relates the text to the sphere of human action. This is Marx's view that false consciousness ends "when what man says is equal to what man does, and when his work is truly equal to his being."[18] If we can envision what we do being commensurate with what we say, and our work being commensurate with who we are, then we have begun to free ourselves from false consciousness. False consciousness assumes the necessity of an incongruity between what we say and what we do, and inequality between our work and our being.

This way of formulating the problem of false consciousness is especially valuable for us here because we are concerned with the relation of texts (what we say) to pastoral action (what we do). Furthermore we want to view the relationship between text and action in the immediate situation as part of the larger world-disclosure reflected in Marx's equation of work to being, which Ricoeur calls Marx's eschatology. In pastoral terms, this is the issue of the relationship between praxis (which we may call pastoral vocation) and being (or pastoral identity). These are issues that will concern us throughout this book.

It may seem odd in a book on pastoral care that we would view Marx as a more important hermeneutician of suspicion than Freud. However, Erik Erikson, himself a Freudian, has said that "probably the most neglected problem in psychoanalysis is the problem of work, in theory as well as in practice: as if the dialectic of the history of ideas had ordered a system of psychological thought which would as resolutely ignore the way in which the individual and his group make a living as Marxism ignores introspective psychology and makes a man's economic position the fulcrum of his acts and thoughts."[19] That Freudian thought has not given enough attention to questions of work and vocation is symptomatic of its neglect of the sphere of human action in general. But these questions simply cannot be ignored in a book on pastoral hermeneutics, especially one whose rationale is based on the similarity between texts and human action.

On the other hand, Erikson's critique of the onesidedness of Marx's perspective points to where the Freudian project of demystification also has special value for us. This concerns Freud's application of the hermeneutics of suspicion to what we say (our oral and written texts). Psychoanalysis entertains the suspicion that much of what we say is not what we mean and that even the speaker is unaware of the discrepancy. Ricoeur's analysis of Freud's position makes it clear that for Freud, the root of this discrepancy is our desires. If we were to say what our real desires are, this might undermine our interpersonal relationships and social institutions. The very survival of human society requires the masking of our real desires, especially our erotic and aggressive desires, and this means learning to speak in ways that conceal or only indirectly reveal our desires. This process of revealing through concealment is one reason our language is polysemic, meaning more than one thing at a time. Thus Freud's assault on false consciousness raises an issue that, as Erikson suggests, Marx does not address. This is the issue that precedes the question of the equality between what we say and what we do, namely, is what we say and do a reflection of what we truly desire? Freud's critique of false consciousness would alert us to the fact that pastoral actions are world-disclosive in the extent to which they reflect true desire. As Erikson points out, Luther came to understand that acting out of real desire was the key to all good work.[20] This is why, in Erikson's view, Luther understood prayer to be the core of Christian identity, for it was in prayer that Luther learned to express his desires freely and directly. This intimate relation between desire and world-disclosure is behind the saying that the Christian life is prayer-in-action. Thus, we need to take this issue of desire very seriously in our concern with the world-disclosiveness of pastoral actions.

We may conclude that there are a number of ways in which readers assume critical distance from a given text. One form of such critical distance is the use of *explanatory methods* to assist in understanding a text. This primarily involves theories, conceptual schemata, and other analytical methods designed to clarify the text's system of meaning. Ricoeur considers this form of critical distance essential for understanding any text because it ensures against a purely subjective, intuitive reading of the text resulting in a *vicious* hermeneutical circle. Another form of critical distance is the method of *demythologization,* which distinguishes those elements of the text that are central to its meaning as a world-disclosing text from those that are unrelated or even inimical to its essential meaning and thus tangential to the reader's appropriation of the text. Possibly, every reader of a given text will engage in some degree of demythologiza-tion, but we assume that this becomes increasingly necessary for readers who do not share the "natural cognitive systems" of the author and the original intended readers. A third form of critical distance is *demystification*, where the reader considers the meaning systems of the text to be essentially false and thus incapable of any true world-disclosure. The reader does not accuse the author of conscious deception but claims that the text reflects a discredited world view. How does the reader know this? Ricoeur suggests that the reader's suspicions are *raised* by the text's social or cultural origins. But it appears that they are *confirmed* through the use of the first form of critical distance, that is, the use of analytical methods to clarify the text's systems of language and meaning. In much the same way that Ricoeur sees a dialectic of similarity-dissimilarity in the structure of metaphorical language, the Marxian is likely to see a dialectic of domination and submission, and the Freudian evidence of concealed or displaced desire, in the language structures of texts they judge to be instances of false consciousness.

These three approaches differ in their degree of critical distance from the text, and each has a different rationale for rejecting a naive understanding of the text. The first approach wants to avoid the naiveté of *intuition*, or a purely subjective reading of the text. The second approach wants to avoid the naiveté of *indiscrimination*, the failure to distinguish between the core world-disclosive meanings of a text and its peripheral meanings. The third wants to avoid the naiveté of *credulity*, or reading a text at face value without concern for the social and cultural attitudes it reflects. All three ways of avoiding naiveté are also appropriate to pastoral action. The primary focus of this study is the first approach, but the others will not be neglected. The second will be illustrated through Ricoeur's dis-tinction between a text's ostensive and world-disclosive meanings. The third will be addressed through attention to the problem of false consciousness as experienced by the pastor.

CONCLUSION

We have addressed a number of hermeneutical issues in this chapter. In some cases their relevance to pastoral concerns is im-mediately apparent. In other cases their relevance will have to be established more clearly as we go along. In a sense, metaphorical thought provides the rationale for this study. For what is being claimed here is that pastoral actions are *like* texts. Furthermore, this study assumes that we are probably more skilled in understanding texts than in understanding pastoral actions. Thus, our experience in understanding the meaning of texts is the "known" that sheds light on efforts to understand the meaning of pastoral actions, the "lesser known." Some readers will question this assumption on the grounds that they understand what they are doing in pastoral care much better than they understand texts they read. This may be true for many individuals. But our task here is to make a contribution to the methodology of pastoral care, and my own conviction is that we are very short on methodologies for understanding what makes pastoral actions meaningful. If hermeneutics can provide such a methodology, it could not have come at a better time.

This does not mean of course that viewing pastoral actions as texts is the only way to view them. Pastoral actions have been compared with other kinds of actions, such as parental, psychotherapeutic, political, and artistic actions. They have also been compared with other kinds of phenomena, such as the growth of an organism or the construction of an edifice. But viewing pastoral actions as texts necessarily focuses our attention on the task of *understanding the meaning of pastoral actions,* and it challenges us to discover how pastoral actions are world-disclosive for those they influence. Admittedly, our metaphor suggests that, in the final analysis, what makes a given pastoral action world-disclosive may be its *dissimilarity* to texts. But we will be in a better position to discover even this fact once we have established that texts and pastoral actions have much in common.

CHAPTER 2

A Hermeneutical Model
for
Pastoral Care

This chapter develops a hermeneutical model for pastoral care. It is based on my discussion of Ricoeur's theory of hermeneutics in chapter 1, supplemented by more sustained analysis of his proposal that meaningful actions are like texts.[1] The basic rationale for this model is the similarity between texts and human action, and the potential that this similarity has for helping us to understand that form of human action we call pastoral care. Because the analogy between texts and human action has fundamental importance for this whole enterprise, our first task is to make a case for the analogy. Fortunately, Ricoeur addresses this very issue in the seminal article indicated above.

THE TEXT AND HUMAN ACTION

What is Ricoeur's rationale for linking a text and meaningful action so that the same approach to understanding a text may be used in understanding human actions? First, Ricoeur points out that "meaningful action" excludes random or inconsequential action and includes only action that is worthy of understanding. Second, meaningful action is more similar to written texts than spoken discourse because it shares many of the traits of the written text. These include:

1. *Like written texts, meaningful action leaves its mark.* Unlike spoken discourse but like written texts, meaningful actions have significance beyond the moment. They have a *content* that can be identified and reidentified and is therefore available for interpretation. They also have *influence* or *force.* Like a text, meaningful action not only "says" something but also "does" something. As texts have impact on their

readers, so meaningful actions have effects on those involved in the action. When a pastor makes a hospital visit to a dying parishioner, the visit has a *content* that may be the object of interpretation, and it has an *influence* on the pastor, the dying patient, and anyone else directly involved in the action.

2. *Like written texts, meaningful action has unintended consequences.* Texts typically have meanings and effects that their authors did not intend. Once the text has left the author's hands and has been acquired by the reader, what the text says matters more than what the author meant to say. In spoken discourse the speaker can quickly correct misstatements and misunderstandings: "That is not what I meant. Let me try to clarify what I'm trying to say." In written discourse efforts to rescue the text from unintended understandings are more difficult. In any dispute over how the text is to be understood, the meaning of the text and not the intentions of the author takes priority. In a similar way, actions usually have meanings and effects their agents did not intend. Supposing a pastor who visited a dying patient reports to members of the family who were not in town at the time that their father was lucid the night he died. By telling them this he hopes to comfort them. He intends that they will be relieved that their father was clear-headed to the very end of his days. But supposing instead that his assurance has the opposite effect. One of the dead man's daughters turns to her sister and says, "See, what did I tell you. I said we should have tried to be at the hospital that night, but you said it wouldn't matter because he would not recognize us." The pastor's intention to provide assurance had the unintended effect of precipitating a painful family dispute. Ricoeur suggests that for most meaningful actions the agent's intention is not the primary issue for understanding their meanings. Actions take on a life of their own and thus become "depsychologized"—the agent's purpose no longer dominates the meaning of the event. For Ricoeur, this raises an important ethical question because the claim "I did not intend *this* to happen" is an insufficient response to the question of responsibility for one's actions.

3. *Like written texts, meaningful action creates a world.* Ricoeur claims that in spoken discourse the "world" the speakers communicate is one they already share. But in written discourse a world is actually opened up for us. Written discourse "projects a world" that is free from the narrowness or limits of the original dialogical situation. Thus "texts speak of possible worlds and of possible ways of orienting oneself in those worlds."[2] In a similar way, meaningful action has

importance beyond its relevance to the initial situation: "An important action, we could say, develops meanings which can be actualized or fulfilled in situations other than the one in which this action occurred."[3] The action reflects the meanings it had when first enacted but in addition opens a world that exceeds these original intended meanings. Thus a couple's initial intention to marry opens up a world which neither explicitly intended at the time. Yet that world is already in the action as a nonostensive reference. It is not that this world is deeply hidden in the action as though the action were a crystal ball that holds all the secrets of what the couple's relationship will come to be in the future. Instead, it is a world that the action projects outward from itself—a possible world and a possible way of orienting themselves to this world.

Unlike random or inconsequential actions, meaningful actions create meanings that are actualized or fulfilled in other situations than the one in which they first occurred. This is also true of many pastoral actions. While some pastoral actions are more like spoken discourse—communicating a world we already share—others open up unintended worlds of meaning and significance. The pastor's report to the daughters of their father's lucidity the night he died had unfortunate consequences he did not intend. But it also opened possible worlds that were not clearly evident at the time. Ricoeur calls this the opening of "new dimensions of our being-in-the-world." Whatever specific form these new "worlds" might take, they would have in common with texts' world-disclosures the fact that they are not limited by the ostensive situation (the death of the women's father) but are free to take hold of other meanings unintentionally disclosed by the action. Now that the daughters are feuding, how might I minister to *that?*

4. *Like written texts, meaningful action is always open to reinterpretation.* In spoken discourse one addresses another person who is present to this situation. Written discourse is not limited to the present situation but is in principle accessible to anyone who knows how to read. Persons removed from the author in space and time may also understand the text. In a similar way, meaningful action is an "open book" which is accessible to "readers" who were not present at the time the action took place. These new readers may discover meanings in the action that were not seen by the original agent or those who were actually present. Thus Ricoeur says that past actions are open to fresh interpretations, and fresh interpretations are most compelling when they reflect not only fresh *thinking* about the action but also

current *praxis*—new *actions* addressed to the original action. (This is like rereading a text. Instead of merely reflecting on a text we once read, it is often valuable to reread the text for better understanding.) In the case we have been discussing, the pastor decided to visit one of the daughters and in the course of the conversation reminded her of her argument with her sister at her father's gravesite. This disclosed a world that he could not have anticipated on the basis of the previous episode, but now emerged in this second pastoral action. A passionate account of the two daughters' conflicts over the years followed. The pastor discovered things from this return visit that he could not have discerned from reflecting further on the meaning of the earlier dispute.

UNDERSTANDING AND EXPLANATION

Besides pointing to these common elements in texts and meaningful action, Ricoeur gives considerable attention in his essay on texts and human actions to what the interpretation of texts has to contribute to interpretation of human actions. He recognizes that hermeneutics originally made a distinction between hermeneutics and those sciences concerned with the study of the natural and social world. In turn, this led to the view that hermeneutics is a science of understanding, while the natural and social sciences are based on explanation. But Ricoeur wants to break this distinction down by showing that the process of understanding includes explanation. He suggests that interpretation of human actions begins with a *guess* as to what the action means, followed by attempts to *validate* this guess, and culminating in *comprehension* of the action. The guess is an act of preunderstanding, the validation of the guess is an act of explanation, and comprehension is an act of understanding in which the action is personally appropriated.

The purpose of the guess is to establish the perspective from which to interpret the action. Since the action is accessible from a variety of perspectives, the guess is the proposal of a given perspective from which to understand the action. Thus, the guess provides a point of entry into the interpretation of the actions. It says, We recognize that the action means many different things, but let us begin here. However, understanding an action begins with a guess but it cannot end there. What is also needed is validation of one's interpretation of what is going on, and this introduces the need for explanatory schemata. The guess establishes the point of entry while the schemata provide hypotheses for further explanation of the action. Such schemata are the counterparts of structural analysis of the language system of texts, or theories, concepts, and models used in the analysis of the text's system of meanings. And because hermeneutics aims at being a general science of interpretation, the same explanatory schemata may be used for both texts and actions. As with texts, so with human action, the schema is not, however, an end in itself. The ultimate goal is to comprehend an action through appropriation of its meaning, and this means gaining an understanding of its world-disclosive power. Thus a guess leads to explanation, which in turn leads to comprehension of the action's world-disclosive power.

MEANINGFUL PASTORAL ACTIONS

By drawing attention to common elements in texts and meaningful action and by noting that texts and meaningful action lend themselves to essentially the same hermeneutical process, Ricoeur provides the basis for connecting hermeneutics and pastoral care. It is axiomatic that pastoral care is centered in *action,* usually toward other persons. This does not always mean persons who are immediately present, because meaningful actions have consequences that are not limited to the immediate situation. Also, this does not mean that our actions are addressed only to human persons; for prayer to God is one of the most meaningful acts of pastoral care. In addition, pastoral care can be action that is directed toward creating or sustaining institutions or movements from which persons will indirectly benefit. There is no question that pastoral care is centered in action. The real question is not whether it is action but whether it is *meaningful* action.

I assume that we are concerned here only with *meaningful* pastoral actions. Our focus is actions that leave their mark, have unintended consequences, disclose a world, and are always open to reinterpretation. This rules out actions that are random or inconsequential even though they may be instances of pastoral interest. "That's a nice tie you're wearing, Fred." "Well, thanks, Pastor, it's nice of you to notice." Pastoral regard? Yes. Fred has been complimented, given positive recognition, and probably experienced a modest boost to his self-esteem. But *meaningful* action? Probably not. It may leave its mark ("Pastor, remember the day you complimented me on my tie?"). It may have unintended consequences ("Pastor, since you

liked my tie so much I bought you one just like it"). It may disclose a
world ("Pastor, you're right, it's a nice tie. But to me it symbolizes
human bondage. Just like your clerical collar"). It may be open to
reinterpretation ("Fred, do you suppose the pastor was teasing you a
little about your tie? I know you like the piano keyboard design but
I'm sure a lot of people wouldn't"). More likely, though, the episode
will not have any of these effects. It will remain what it was intended
to be—a pleasant exchange. The kinds of action we are concerned
with in this study are meaningful pastoral actions, and I will assume
that a pastoral action is meaningful if it consists of these four elements.

A HERMENEUTICAL MODEL
FOR PASTORAL CARE

Having established what kinds of pastoral action concern us here,
I want to begin constructing a hermeneutical model for pastoral care
based on Ricoeur's hermeneutical theory, supplemented by E. D.
Hirsch's theories of interpretation. The purpose of this model is
ultimately to assist us in our efforts to understand pastoral actions, to
get at what a given pastoral action means. In developing this model, I
will be concerned with the various factors involved in acquiring such
understanding.

There are various ways to construct a model. One that I considered is the model of the flow chart. Such a model would view
understanding pastoral action as a process whose various stages may
be identified and labeled. This flow chart would be circular in nature
because as we saw in chapter 1 the process of understanding is a
hermeneutical circle beginning and ending with the interpreter. But
I decided against the flow chart model because it creates a very
artificial structure, especially in an implied causality between stages
in the process. Flow charts create the impression that one stage of the
process causes the next, and so forth. This may have some validity in
social institutions where lines of communication and responsibility
are carefully drawn. But this is not what is generally involved in
understanding an action. While there is overall movement from
guess to explanation to comprehension, understanding an action is
more an event than a series of steps. It may be viewed as a process but
not one that follows a strict causal pattern.

Instead of the flow chart I will be proposing a somewhat more
loosely constructed model. It will take into account all the major
factors involved in understanding a text, and then identify their

counterparts in the context of pastoral action. I think of this as a translation model where the terms of one language system (text) are translated into the terms of another language system (pastoral action). The question is: What are the major factors involved in understanding a text, and what are their counterparts in pastoral action?

THE PASTOR'S INTENTIONALITY

First, there is the fact that texts are partly the effect of an author's intentions but they are always more than this. They have meanings that the author did not intend or envision when the text was being written. When we translate this fact into the context of pastoral action, we can say that pastoral actions also have effects that the pastor did not intend, and meanings that were not envisioned when the action was initiated. The gap between the pastor's conscious intentions and what actually resulted may need to be addressed if there is reason to suspect that deliberate deception is involved, as when a pastoral action is not at all what the pastor purports it to be. But the action and not the author's conscious intention is our primary focus. Does this mean that the pastor's intentions are unimportant? No, but it does mean that the intentionality of the pastor is actually better revealed through the action itself than the pastor's conscious intentions. This is not because we have reason to suspect the pastor of misrepresenting these intentions (except in clear cases of deliberate deception). It is simply that even as authors are known by their texts, pastors are known by their actions. Furthermore, even as authors are held responsible for their texts and not for their conscious intentions, so pastors are held responsible for their actions and not for what they thought they were doing.

Thus, our hermeneutical model makes a distinction between the pastor's conscious intentions and the intentionality revealed through the pastoral action itself. It does not neglect the former, especially in cases where the action is not at all what the pastor purports it to be. But it clearly focuses on the latter. In this sense, our model, like Ricoeur's hermeneutics, is "depsychologized." It does not engage in intense probing of the conscious or unconscious intentions of the pastor. But this does not mean that we take no interest in the pastor or that our understanding of the action is psychologically naive. Regarding the pastor, our model takes seriously the biblical view that "by their fruits you shall know them," and that Jesus became known to his fellow travelers "in the breaking of the bread." So when we focus on pastoral actions we are not dismissing the pastors involved, but anticipating that they will become known to us through their actions. Similarly, psychological insights are not applied to the conscious intentions of the pastor (unless they invite our suspicion) but toward understanding the action itself. For a pastoral hermeneutic that gives primacy to the action, this use of psychology does not diminish but actually increases psychology's importance.

NO PRIVILEGED INTERPRETERS

Second, a text may have many different sets of readers. But one important distinction is between the original readers for whom it was intended and subsequent readers who have different motivations for reading the text. Ricoeur's hermeneutical theory says that the original readers do not have privileged status in terms of understanding the text. When we translate this view into the pastoral context, we make a similar point. It cannot be said that only the pastor and those who were physically present at the time of the action are in a position to understand what the action means. In fact, it is very likely that other persons to whom the action is subsequently reported will see meanings in the action that were not perceived by the persons involved. This fact provides a rationale for the pedagogical model used in clinical pastoral education, where verbatim accounts of pastoral actions are interpreted by other students, pastors, and clinical supervisors who were not actually present. It often happens in such sessions that the pastors who wrote the verbatim accounts discover that they have introduced meanings into the text of which they were themselves unaware, and that other persons are able to discern meanings in the action which were not directly reported.

Thus, our hermeneutical model would reject the idea that those who were directly involved in the action have a privileged status as far as understanding the action is concerned. They usually have greater personal investment in the action. But this investment does not in itself afford a privileged status. As a text may be understood by anyone who has the ability to read, so a pastoral action may be understood by anyone who has reasonable access to it.

PASTORAL ACTIONS AS
WORLD-DISCLOSIVE

Third, there is the fact that texts have two kinds of meaning. They have meanings relating to the immediate situation which the author and original readers understand and have some investment in. They also have meanings that transcend the immediate situation and disclose a world that is essentially free from it. Of the two kinds of meanings, the second is by far the more important because these are the meanings that enable the text to have more universal significance. When translated into the pastoral context, this fact suggests that pastoral actions also have two kinds of meaning, one relating to the immediate situation and the other to their capacity to disclose a world that is larger than the immediate situation. It also suggests that we should interpret the action not only for its effects in the immediate situation but also for its world-disclosive potential. Our hermeneutical model makes a distinction between the pastoral action's immediate effects and its world-disclosive potential, and it gives greater emphasis to the latter.

But how does it attend to the world-disclosive character of the pastoral action? What does it look for? Our earlier discussion of Ricoeur's hermeneutical theory indicates that we should give particular attention to the *genre* or *form* of the pastoral action and to its *metaphorical content*. As we have seen, the form or genre of a text plays a very significant role in determining its possible world-disclosures. The text's metaphorical content is also extremely important for its world-disclosive possibilities, because metaphorical language is the bridge between the ostensive references of the text and those that disclose a world. It contributes to such disclosure by using the known world (or immediate situation) as a screen through which we glimpse the lesser known world (or world disclosed).

Much the same can be said for pastoral actions. The *genre* or *form* of the pastoral action plays a very decisive role in determining what kinds of world-disclosures are possible. Once we know the form of the pastoral action we can begin to understand what kinds of world-disclosures are possible and what kinds are not. This does not mean, however, simply *labeling* the form (for example, grief counseling). It means becoming familiar with its structure and processes, and knowing how it works. It means getting inside the form in much the way an author gets inside it by writing a text that employs it. We learn what kinds of world-disclosures are possible for a given form by working with it, by experimenting with it, by becoming intimately acquainted with what it can and cannot do.

But the form is not the whole picture. The *metaphorical content* of the pastoral action is also very important because it concerns the meanings of a specific action and thus its own unique possibilities for world-disclosure. While the form can tell us what kinds of world-disclosure we might expect from this action, the metaphorical content screens out certain of these possible world-disclosures so that what remains has clearer focus, intensity, and transforming power. To illustrate this, consider the following pastoral action: Michael, a pastoral trainee in a hospital, visited Mr. Kern, a cancer patient in very critical condition.[4] When Michael entered the room, Mr. Kern mistook him for a doctor because he was wearing a white coat. When Michael's actual status was clarified he proceeded to inform Mr. Kern why he had come:

> I just want to say hello to you. I want to let you know that we're around and that we'll be happy to help in any way we can. The chaplain's office answers on extension 2765, and in case you are interested, there are services here on Sunday—several ecumenical and one Mass for Catholics.

To this Mr. Kern simply responded, "I am Jewish." Michael informed Mr. Kern that a rabbi makes regular visits to the hospital and asked, "Could I call him for you?" Mr. Kern said, "Please do not. I would prefer not to bother him or anyone," and then asked Michael to leave because "I do not care to talk." Michael indicated that he understood but said he would still like to drop by occasionally "just to see how things are with you." Mr. Kern replied:

> You would indeed be doing me a very great favor ... if you and everyone else would leave me entirely alone. My own family, except for my wife, does not come to see me. I have told my daughter not to come. I don't want her to see me in this condition. Yet people insist. Even a dying animal—a dying animal—can crawl off by itself to die. I repeat: You will be doing me a favor if you leave—and do not return.

Michael left. Later, in his room, he wrote, "I feel as if I have just been kicked in the stomach."

Formally, this pastoral action falls into the genre of care for the sick and dying. Its potential world-disclosures are quite different from those of premarital counseling, pastoral intervention in the case of alcoholism or drug abuse, and so forth. Its potential world-disclosures will thus have their roots in the immediate situation of a man facing imminent death. On the other hand, they can free themselves from the narrowness of this immediate situation by projecting a world in which death is overcome ("O death where is thy victory?") or rendered impotent ("O death where is thy sting?"). In turn, the metaphorical *content* of this conversation provides clues to the specific nature of this world-disclosure. Mr. Kern's metaphorical description of himself as a wounded animal who only wants to be allowed to crawl off by himself and die suggests that he wants to maintain a personal sense of dignity to the end, even if this means the loss of virtually all interpersonal contacts. This projects a world in which death loses its sting when it is not allowed to strip its victim of his essential dignity. This is from the perspective of the patient. For the pastor, the episode discloses a clash of worlds between the patient's desire to die in solitary dignity and Michael's conviction that Mr. Kern's greater need is for companionship as he walks through the valley of the shadow of death. Like the parables of Jesus, this episode leaves the pastor with an uneasy tension between the conventional view to which he was oriented when he came into the room ("This man needs the kind of companionship I can offer") and the disorienting view expressed by the dying patient himself ("You will be doing me a great favor if you leave and do not return").

Thus, our hermeneutical model focuses on the world-disclosive aspects of a pastoral action, and seeks to get at these by concerning itself with the form of a given action and its metaphorical content.

UNDERSTANDING AS
PERSONAL APPROPRIATION

Fourth, there is the fact that the hermeneutical process is in the hands of the reader throughout. The author produces the text but the hermeneutical process does not begin until the reader enters into the task of understanding it. This process is then completed when the reader appropriates the world-disclosures of the text. Thus the hermeneutical process begins and ends with the reader. It moves through the objectivity of the text but comes back at the end to the subjectivity of the reader. When this understanding of the hermeneutical process is translated into the pastoral context, we see that the pastoral action is completed only when it has been understood (not just initiated), and that such understanding entails personal appropriation of the action's world-disclosures. This means that a given pastoral action might be completed weeks, months, or even years after its enactment because personal appropriation of its meaning is not necessarily immediate.

But who does this appropriating? Who are the persons who may be interpreted by the action? Following Ricoeur's view that texts are accessible to anyone who knows how to read, our hermeneutical model does not arbitrarily restrict this group of potential appropriators of the pastoral action. It may include, for example, the person or persons for whom the action was expressly intended, other persons who were present, persons indirectly influenced by the action, persons to whom it was reported secondhand, and the pastor who initiated the action. Often the person who is most likely to make such a personal appropriation of the action is the pastor involved. In such cases the pastor's perspective has shifted from author to reader, from concern with what he or she did to what the action now discloses. Because appropriation of a text means orienting oneself to its world-disclosures, it may well result in a new approach to ministry.

On the other hand, few pastors would find ministry very satisfying if they were the only ones for whom their pastoral actions were world-disclosive. Pastoral actions need to be disclosive for other persons as well, whether the persons for whom the action was initiated or persons who are indirectly affected by the action. Furthermore, we anticipate that persons for whom such actions are world-disclosive are those who are able to see how the action projects a world beyond its immediate setting. This means being able to attend not just to what literally took place, but to those possibilities the action projects.

What are the signs that an individual has appropriated a given pastoral action? Our hermeneutical model assumes that it will be reflected in some reorientation of their lives. This need not be highly dramatic, but it should be meaningful or significant. It may be reflected in various kinds of changes, including perceptual, behavioral, cognitive, and emotional changes. It may result in changes in values, personal commitment, life goals, and fundamental convictions. Our hermeneutical model does not specify the kind or degree of reorientation. But it does affirm that such changes are the effects of a process of understanding where we are not just interpreters of the action, but interpreted by it. Thus, whatever its short- or long-range effects, the pastoral action "interprets" the individual. And whatever else it may mean, to be interpreted means an increase in self-awareness. More on this point in a moment.

PASTORAL ACTIONS AS DYNAMIC PROCESS

Fifth, by noting that Jesus' parables take us through a pattern of orientation to disorientation to reorientation, Ricoeur suggests that texts have an internal dynamic. In the case of narratives, this dynamic is carried by the plot structure. Pastoral actions that are meaningful also have a plot structure, or internal dynamic. A hermeneutical model that seeks to gain insight into the meaning of such pastoral actions needs to address itself to these three factors, with each building on the previous one in an essentially circular process: (1) identifying the basic *dynamic* of the pastoral action; (2) making a *diagnostic* assessment of the action; and (3) determining whether and in what ways the action is *disclosive*.

If, for example, we wanted to get at the meaning of the Michael–Mr. Kern action, we would first want to identify what is the basic dynamic in this encounter. Knowledge of psychodynamics can be especially helpful at this stage. We might, for example, view Mr. Kern's dynamics in terms of Erikson's eighth stage of the life cycle, integrity vs. despair, and Michael's dynamics in terms of Erikson's fifth stage of intimacy vs. isolation. In the dynamic interplay between the two "characters" in the story, both are personally threatened. Michael is threatened by Mr. Kern's isolation while Mr. Kern is threatened by Michael's efforts to break through his despair. Much more could be said about these dynamics (and undoubtedly would be said if this pastoral action were presented in a clinical pastoral education seminar), but this brief example indicates how identification of the action's internal dynamics might proceed.

Having identified the basic dynamic of the action, our hermeneutical model would propose moving to the diagnostic stage. It would attempt to evaluate or assess the dynamics in the episode, both individual and interpersonal and, where relevant, psychosocial.[5] A valuable resource here might be the theological themes developed by Paul W. Pruyser, or the biblical themes formulated by William B. Oglesby, Jr.[6] With Pruyser, we might say that Mr. Kern lacks "awareness of the holy" and rebuffs Michael because he is professionally identified with the holy, while Michael is having difficulty finding grounds for "communion" between himself and Mr. Kern; thus far, his efforts are too instrumental and programmatic. With Oglesby, we might say that the dynamic interplay here involves the biblical theme of initiative and freedom (Mr. Kern has the right to refuse Michael's pastoral initiatives), while Michael is presented with the opportunity to help Mr. Kern find a more perfect, less defensive freedom. Should this occur, the focus of Michael's ministry to Mr. Kern might then open an even deeper theme implicit here, Oglesby's theme of death and rebirth. While these two resources, Pruyser and Oglesby, are essentially theological, they are informed by psychological insights. Thus the diagnostic assessment of a pastoral action is generally informed by a combination of theological and psychological insights.

Having viewed the action diagnostically, our next step is to determine whether and how the action is disclosive. Here, as noted earlier, the *form* and *metaphorical content* of the action are especially critical. By identifying the form of the pastoral action, we are able to make an educated "guess" as to what kind of disclosure is possible or likely. In this case, the form is the hospital visit to a patient who is apparently dying. This form sets the parameters of the action's disclosive possibilities. As to metaphorical content, our hermeneutical model is especially concerned with how a pastoral action contributes to increased self-awareness. Therefore, in exploring the disclosiveness of a pastoral action, we will be especially attentive to those metaphorical contents that reveal something about the individual's self-awareness. A good example is Mr. Kern's description of himself as a "dying animal" who wants to crawl off by himself and die. Such self-metaphors are central to the action's disclosiveness. In addition to these more occasional self-metaphors, there are also self-metaphors that have gained the status of models. As Sallie McFague points out, models are metaphors with unusual staying power, their permanence attributable to the fact that they comprise a whole cluster of metaphors.[7] In chapter 4, I will discuss three such self-metaphors (the responsible, believable, and accessible selves), and will propose that these be used in evaluating an individual's growth in self-awareness through a given pastoral action. These more enduring self-metaphors may be less explicit than Mr. Kern's "dying animal" metaphor, but they are part of the deeper structure of the dynamic process, and one or more of them can usually be discerned. Often, the more occasional metaphor like "dying animal" is a valuable clue to the deeper and more enduring "model" of the self.

Why does our hermeneutical model view growth in self-awareness as the primary effect of a pastoral action's world-disclosure? The basic *hermeneutical* rationale for this emphasis on self-awareness is the simple fact that, in approaching a text or action, one is interpreted by it. To be "interpreted by" a pastoral action is, in effect, to become more self-aware. The basic *religious* rationale for this view is that self-awareness is the basic quality we share with God; it is what justifies our claim to be created in the image of God. As Erik Erikson points out, God is an eternal center of awareness who confirms our claims to self-awareness. As he puts it, to have a sense of "self" or "I" awareness

> is nothing less than the verbal assurance according to which I feel that I am the center of awareness in a universe of experience in which I have a coherent identity. . . . The counterplayer of the "I" therefore can be, strictly speaking, only the deity who . . . is Himself endowed with an eternal numinousness.[8]

Thus, our hermeneutical model is especially attentive to increase in self-awareness as an effect of the disclosive power of a meaningful pastoral action.

Pastoral theologians have long recognized that reflection on pastoral actions involves identifying their *dynamics* and making a *diagnostic* assessment in terms of these dynamics. Our hermeneutical model, guided by Ricoeur's concern for the world-disclosiveness of meaningful actions, adds a third important concern: the *disclosiveness* of the pastoral action. A complete "reflection" on a given action will give serious attention to its disclosiveness, since this is the ultimate purpose of the pastoral action.

UNDERSTANDING THROUGH CONCEPTUAL SCHEMATA

Sixth, Ricoeur emphasizes the need for methods of interpretation to clarify the text's language and meaning systems. Such methods may be supported by theories, conceptual schemata or models derived from the humanities, social sciences, and even natural sciences. We saw, for example, his use of Lévi-Strauss to clarify the text's language system. We also saw his use of metaphor theory to enable him to move from the language system into the meaning of the text. When this feature of the hermeneutical process is translated into the pastoral context we can readily see what it entails. It means that we also need conceptual models for interpretation of pastoral actions. Otherwise, our interpretation lacks sufficient objectivity. I find E. D. Hirsch's views in this regard a helpful supplement to Ricoeur, especially Hirsch's discussion of four general approaches to understanding a text. These include intuitionism, positivism, perspectivism, and schematism. Among these four Hirsch favors schematism because it recognizes the importance of conceptual models for understanding texts and their meaning. Since these four approaches are also relevant to pastoral action, I will briefly comment on Hirsch's discussion of each.[9]

Intuitionism. This position conceives the text as an occasion for direct communion with another person, normally the text's author. Hirsch calls this approach intuitive "because even though it is mediated at first by words, it is not constrained, in the end, by their form."[10] He recognizes that understanding ultimately means "transcending" the text. For the intuitionist, however, the form in which the words are expressed has little if any effect on the nature of the communion that takes place. In contrast to this view, Ricoeur's discussion of biblical genres shows that the revelatory possibilities of these texts are determined by the form of the text. Each genre allows for transcendence of the text, but each genre determines what form this transcendence takes. Thus the major argument against intuitionism as a method for understanding texts is that it minimizes the mediating function of the form in whatever direct communion the text *makes possible* (whether between persons, ourselves and others, or, where the text is a sacred text like the Bible or prayer book, between ourselves and God).

Positivism. This position says that we should take the words of a text at face value because the words speak their own meaning. In this view there is no distinction between a text's verbal medium and the meaning it represents. Thus it claims that by analyzing the language system of the text we can identify the text's meaning. Hirsch agrees with positivism's view that there must be some direct correlation between the language system of a text and its meaning. But he contends that a given collection of words may yield more than one set of meanings and thus positivism exaggerates the "coercive power of linguistic form."[11] He cites irony as an example of the same language system having multiple meanings, because its presence or absence changes nothing in the text except its fundamental meaning. Thus the meanings of a text are not revealed solely by its language system. Additional interpretive steps are required to identify these meanings.

Perspectivism. This approach grows out of a modern skepticism regarding the possibility of correct interpretation of a text. Its psychological version says that a given text cannot mean the same for me as it does for you because we look at it from different subjective standpoints. Its historical version makes the same argument for interpreters who stand at different points in cultural space and time. Both stress that interpretation is relative to the interpreter. Hirsch agrees with the perspectivist view that any given text may yield different interpretations. But he takes issue with perspectivism when it presents its views dogmatically, claiming that there can be no general agreement among interpreters regarding the meaning of a text. He contends that perspectivism places so much emphasis on the interpreters and their differences that it fails to take seriously enough the "self-identity" of the text. Using visual perception as an analogy, he argues that two observers can see the very same thing even though their perspective on it differs. Thus it is possible for persons coming at the text from differing perspectives to arrive at a common understanding of it. He does not base this argument on the claim that interpreters of the text might reach a consensus through social process, but on the fact that a text is the same however we approach it, and this self-identity of the text can be recognized whatever our angle of vision.

Schematism. This approach, which Hirsch prefers, takes the view that interpretation of texts "follows a general pattern which governs our coming to cognitive terms with our world."[12] We approach texts in much the same way as any other object we want to come to know. Hirsch is impressed by the fact that across the whole spectrum of arts and sciences there is general agreement that we approach the object of our inquiry with cognitive predispositions. What Heidegger, in setting forth his hermeneutical model, called "the priority of preunderstanding is described by developmental psychologists as the primacy of the schema; by Gombrich, in art history, as the primacy of the genre; by cognitive theorists (particularly those concerned with scientific knowledge) as the primacy of the hypothesis," and so forth. Hirsch acknowledges that a model is not just the same as a type, a type exactly the same as a genre, a genre precisely the same as a hypothesis. But each of these has important features in common, especially that of establishing a set or range of expectations as one addresses the object of interest or study. Following the cognitive-developmental theorist Jean Piaget, Hirsch refers to these predispositions as corrigible or correctable schemata, and says that we approach all objects of cognitive inquiry, including texts, by means of such schemata. Such a "schema sets up a range of predictions or expectations, which if fulfilled confirms the schema, but if not fulfilled causes us to revise it."[13] What results is a "making-matching, constructive-corrective process."[14]

When applied to texts, the schema with which we address the text establishes certain expectations. If these are met the schema is confirmed. If not it needs correction. But in any case we do not address the text without cognitive predispositions. Hirsch considers this schema to be so important to the hermeneutical process that for him, a general theory of interpretation is essentially a theory of correctable schemata. This means that explanation through *validation* has a certain primacy in the interpretive process. Understanding occurs when we take the schema that we have constructed and test to see whether the text validates it or requires us to alter it.

Hirsch's analyses of these four hermeneutical approaches are valuable for our own hermeneutical model because essentially the same critiques apply to their use in understanding pastoral actions. As for texts, so for pastoral actions, the purpose of such approaches should be to place the process of understanding on a firm objective footing. Let us review these four approaches with this requirement in mind.

Intuitionism. In recent decades, considerable progress has been made in pastoral care as the various forms of pastoral care are being identified and their uniqueness highlighted. Against this progress, the intuitionist conceives pastoral care as direct communion between persons and considers the form of pastoral care actions to be irrelevant to the realization of this objective. The pastor who says, "The purpose of pastoral care is simply to be 'present' to another person" reflects this intuitionist position. For the intuitionist it does not matter what the form of the pastoral action may be; what does matter is that the form not be allowed to become a barrier to achieving direct communion with another person.

Against this view, our hermeneutical model says that the form of the action has considerable influence on what the action can mean, especially with regard to its world-disclosive possibilities. An action identified as grief counseling will have different world-disclosive possibilities from an action identified as marriage counseling. I say this in full recognition of the fact that death and divorce may have much in common.[15] Moreover, in cases where the pastor initiating these actions is one and the same person, the form and not the person is the primary determining factor in what will be the world-disclosive possibilities in each case. It is vitally important therefore for the pastor to understand the form of the action and its world-disclosive possibilities. And it is equally important that we avoid genre errors, such as arbitrarily applying the methods of one form to another, or viewing all pastoral actions as merely variations of a single preferred form.

Positivism. A positivistic approach to pastoral action has the virtue of taking the action itself seriously. As with the textual positivist's focus on the language system of the text, the pastoral positivist is concerned with the empirical facts of the pastoral action.

Unfortunately, the positivist fails to recognize that the meaning of the action is not limited to "what happened." In fact, we do not really begin to understand an action's meaning until we focus on its world-disclosive aspects, on "what *may* be happening." But positivists are unable to focus on the action's world-disclosive aspects because they take the view that the action yields a single meaning, not multiple and potentially conflicting meanings. Awareness of the multiple meanings of the action is the first step toward recognizing its world-disclosive possibilities. The positivist's failure to see that pastoral actions have multiple meanings is often reflected in a reluctance to follow up on this action. The action has occurred, its meaning is clear, and that's it: "If you want me to go back and see Mr. Kern again, I'll go. But as far as I'm concerned it was a simple matter of his wanting to be left alone." This reluctance to follow up on an action, to gain more understanding of it, is frequently justified on the grounds that "I don't want to get involved in a lot of psychologizing. Maybe Mr. Kern did not mean exactly what he said or meant more than he said, but how should I know? I'm a pastor, not a clinical psychologist." Against this positivistic view, our hermeneutical model says that it is not a question of whether one chooses to be "psychological" or not, but whether one accepts the premise of hermeneutical theory that discourse has multiple meanings.

In short, intuitionism and positivism have an inadequate approach to the world-disclosive possibilities of a pastoral action. Intuitionism fails to take seriously enough the effect of the form of the action on its world-disclosive possibilities, while positivism rejects the basic premise behind the claim for these world-disclosive possibilities, namely, that pastoral actions have multiple meanings.

Perspectivism. In recent years perspectivism has been a very influential approach in pastoral theology.[16] It is encouraging, therefore, that Hirsch does not challenge the basic idea that we address texts from various perspectives. Furthermore, Ricoeur suggests that our perspective on a text may guide our initial "guess" as to what the text means. When translated to the pastoral situation, this suggests that perspective-taking has considerable value in *initiating* the process of understanding a pastoral action. This approach has problems, however, when it is taken to be sufficient as a general hermeneutical method. The basic problem with perspectivism is that it does not take the "self-identity" of the action seriously enough. It gives insufficient attention to the fact that meanings inhere in the actions themselves, and these meanings can be recognized from whatever perspective one chooses to gain entry into the action. This does not mean that everyone who has an interest in a given pastoral action will understand it in the same way. Certainly, differences will arise when it comes to personal appropriation of the action. What this does mean, however, is that the possibility of such common understanding is not ruled out in advance. Moreover, the reason for this possibility is not that those interested in the action may come to such common understanding because they happen to be agreeable persons, but because the action has its own objective reality and thus yields certain inescapable meanings that are evident to all who have interest in the action whatever their unique perspective may be.

In recent years the perspectivist view in pastoral theology has been useful as a method for challenging a positivistic interpretation of pastoral actions. Against positivism's view that actions have a single meaning based on "what happened," it has argued for the view that actions have multiple meanings. It has tended to attribute the multiple meanings of the action, however, to the multiple perspectives of the interpreters, thus failing to recognize that the action and not the interpreters is the ultimate source of its multiple meanings. If these multiple meanings are located in the action, then they are objectively there and not merely a function of the perspectives of the interpreters.

Thus, perspectivism is important because it provides us with our initial guesses toward understanding the pastoral action. The pastor who actually engaged in the action will make different guesses from those of the person for whom it was intended, or from those of peers, clinical supervisors, other professionals, or other parishioners who may have interest in the action. What guesses one makes will have considerable effect on how one initially understands the action. But our hermeneutical model emphasizes that these guesses ultimately come up against the action itself and they will be changed and modified as a result of this encounter with the "self-identity" of the action. Ultimately, the perspective of the interpreter is not as important as the action's self-identity.

Schematism. This is the approach that Hirsch favors and it is the one that our hermeneutical model also finds most valuable. However, I consider the perspectivist approach to be valuable also because it enables us to guess at the meaning of actions. Also, I do not believe that hermeneutics should be virtually reduced to a theory of correctable schemata. Such schemata are a vital element in the hermeneutical process, but as Ricoeur points out, this process ends with personal appropriation, the orienting of one's life to the world-disclosures of the action. Correctable schemata will affect but do not ultimately determine this eventual orientation.

For a hermeneutics of pastoral action, schematism is important because it avoids the extreme relativism of the perspectivist approach. Instead of viewing the hermeneutical process as one in which the meanings of the text are relative to the perspectives of the interpreters, this approach says that the cognitive schemata of the interpreters are tested against the objective reality of the text in a "making-matching, constructive-corrective process." Of course, no hermeneutical approach can avoid relativism altogether. Positivism has tried, but at the expense of reducing the text's meaning system to its language system. Schematism, however, reduces relativism by emphasizing the objective reality of the text. While a text is always open to reinterpretation, there are limits to what it can mean. Some interpretations the text simply will not allow. They do violence to its meaning. And like other violent acts (murder, rape), they rob their victims of their self-identity. Thus, we are free to try out all manner of conceptual schemata on a given text, but the text is the final arbiter of what schemata are appropriate. Ricoeur's hermeneutical theory provides one absolutely essential criterion in this regard: The conceptual schema must enable us to transcend the limits of the text's ostensive situation and identify its world-disclosive possibilities.

The same principle applies to the hermeneutics of pastoral action. Our hermeneutical model contends that to understand a given pastoral action in a manner that is not critically naive, we need to resist our intuitionist and positivist impulses, and to go beyond perspectivism. This entails the use of conceptual schemata to inform our understanding of the action. These will always be correctable schemata, meaning that they will always be subject to revision, modification, and even replacement with more adequate schemata. But they are necessary if we want to get beyond the guessing that perspectivism makes possible, to a more systematic understanding of the action itself, especially its world-disclosive possibilities.

In chapter 3 I will illustrate the use of such conceptual schemata in the interpretation of pastoral actions, so I will not discuss the merits of schematism any further at this point. However, I would like to point out that while hermeneutics cuts across the traditional division between the humanities and the natural and social sciences, and therefore our conceptual schemata may be derived from virtually any discipline, psychology has enjoyed a privileged status in pastoral care, and its conceptual schemata have had greater value for pastoral care than those of other scholarly disciplines. Our model reflects this psychological emphasis by focusing on the contribution of pastoral actions to increase in self-awareness. (This point will be elaborated on in chapter 4.) At the same time, our emphasis here on pastoral *actions* invites greater attention in pastoral care to the sociology of action.[17]

PASTORAL INTEGRITY

Seventh, our hermeneutical model of pastoral action addresses the problem of false consciousness. As we saw in chapter 1, the charge of false consciousness is not directed toward the author of the text. The author is not being accused of consciously false or deceptive intentions. Rather, those who raise the issue of false consciousness are contending that the text is rooted in convictions and values which they suspect are fundamentally false perceptions of reality. The real culprit is not the author but the culture that produces the author, and it is this culture's assumptions about reality that they wish to expose.

Some critics of the Christian community, at least its traditionally dominant forms, would say that all pastoral actions are instances of false consciousness because the Christian community is wedded to cultural convictions and values that are based on false perceptions of reality. Ultimately, an adequate hermeneutical model for pastoral care would need to address this critique. But for the purposes of this study, I have chosen to address the problem of false consciousness on a more modest level, namely, false consciousness as experienced by the individual pastor. This is essentially the issue Alastair V. Campbell addresses in his discussion of "pastoral integrity."[18] Our approach to this issue of pastoral integrity is informed by Marx's and Freud's critiques of false consciousness. This means we will want to address the following questions in our efforts to understand a given pastoral action: (1) Is there an essential congruence between the pastor's intentionality in the action itself and the action's appropriation by others? (2) Is the pastor's praxis, as reflected in this action, a true reflection of his or her pastoral self-understanding? (3) Do the world-disclosive possibilities of the action address the fundamental human desires of the individuals for whom they are intended? The first two questions focus on the pastor's vocation, and thus address Marx's concerns. The third focuses on the relation between desire and world-disclosure, and thus addresses Freud's concerns.

The first of these two questions is not addressed by investigating the relationship between the pastor's *conscious* intentions and the pastoral action. Rather, it involves focusing on the pastoral action itself, and exploring the relationship between the pastor's intentionality as revealed through the action and the meanings the action has for those who appropriate it. There could well be a discrepancy between the pastor's conscious intentions and the pastoral action, and yet an essential congruence between the intentionality of the action and its appropriation. If such congruence exists, we would judge the action evidence of pastoral integrity.

The second of these two questions is addressed by looking for a consistency between the pastor's *praxis* as reflected in a whole series of pastoral actions and the *pastoral self-understanding* out of which the pastor works. We would get at the pastor's *praxis* by exploring the intentionality-meaning patterns of a series of representative pastoral actions. *Pastoral self-understandings* are notoriously difficult to identify, but one of the most valuable resources for this are the pastoral models formulated by pastoral theologians in recent years. There is the shepherd model (Seward Hiltner), the wounded healer (Henri Nouwen), and the wise fool (Alastair Campbell drawing on previous work by Heije Faber and others).[19] The assumption behind such models is that they inform the pastors' self-understanding as they engage in the praxis of ministry. If the action reveals an essential congruence between a pastor's praxis and pastoral self-understanding, we would judge it to be evidence of pastoral integrity. (In the following chapter, I will be exploring the relationship between praxis and pastoral self-understanding in detail, using these pastoral models to clarify this relationship.)

The third question addresses the integrity issue by focusing on the effects of the action on those who appropriate it. I do not assume that our fundamental human desires are necessarily good and wholesome. But I do assume that pastoral actions will not be world-disclosive unless they relate to fundamental human desires, such as Mr. Kern's intense desire to maintain his basic personal dignity to the end of his days. Such desires need to be studied for their ethical and theological validity, which we will begin to do in chapter 4 through our discussion of how the world-disclosures of pastoral action may contribute to *personal* self-understanding. For the moment, however, my concern is with the role that desire plays in the world-disclosiveness of a pastoral action. Pastoral actions that do not address real desires have little chance of being meaningful; in turn, a ministry that is largely devoid of meaningful pastoral actions lacks integrity. In chapters 3 and 4, I will discuss a case where a pastoral action did address the desires of the individual for whom it was primarily intended, and therefore had world-disclosive possibilities for her.

CONCLUSION

In this chapter I have presented a hermeneutical model for understanding pastoral actions based on Ricoeur and supplemented by Hirsch. There are two major issues that will require further exploration in the next two chapters. One is the role that conceptual schemata play in our effort to understand pastoral actions. I will discuss this issue more thoroughly in chapter 3, and illustrate it with a case study in chapter 4. In this discussion I will attempt to show that good conceptual schemata help us to understand the meaning of individual pastoral actions within the larger context of the pastor's praxis and pastoral self-understanding. The second issue is the assertion that meaningful pastoral actions are world-disclosive. This raises certain fundamental questions that I will explore further in chapter 5. How do we know when an action has been world-disclosive for someone? And what are the anticipated effects of an individual's appropriation of such world-disclosures? To answer these questions, we will need to explore more fully our claim that the key to the pastoral action's world-disclosiveness is its form and metaphorical content.

CHAPTER 3

Conceptual Schemata
in
Pastoral Hermeneutics

Conceptual schemata used in the interpretation of texts are not simply imposed on the text in cookie-cutter fashion. Rather, there is a reciprocity between schema and text involving making and matching, constructing and correcting. The schemata are correctable. Their purpose is to assist us in penetrating the text's systems of meaning once it has been initially opened up by the guess afforded by our particular perspective. Conceptual schemata serve the very same purpose in the case of pastoral action. Our perspective enables us to approach the action, but the conceptual schema enables us to penetrate its systems of meaning.

SELECTING A SCHEMA

Later in this chapter I will provide an example of a conceptual schema applicable to pastoral actions. But first I want to offer criteria for selecting a conceptual schema. This is not a complete list of possible criteria, but these five are certainly central ones.

1. Does the conceptual schema permit an appropriate critical distance on the pastoral action? Some conceptual schemata are so closely allied with the conscious intention behind the pastoral action that they do not allow us to focus on the meaning of the pastoral action itself. One major purpose of a conceptual schema is to enable us to shift from the perspective of *initiator* of the action to *interpreter*. One way to ensure that this happens is by selecting a conceptual schema that has no apparent relevance to the immediate situation of the pastoral action, but does have relevance to its meaning. For example, James Dittes uses psychological theories and research findings on the motivations behind racial and ethnic prejudice to under-

stand pastors' professed aversion to church administration.[1] The conceptual schema has no apparent relevance to the immediate situation (church administration), but it proves to be highly relevant to its systems of meanings. Dittes shows that the same motivations that underlie racial and ethnic prejudice also underlie pastors' professed aversion to church administration. A conceptual schema derived from business administration would have had more direct relevance to the immediate situation, but less relevance to the *meaning* of the actions involved. Thus the schema need not relate to the situational aspects of the action. In fact, there is greater likelihood that we will focus on the meanings of the action if it does not. The real question in selecting a conceptual schema is whether it promises to penetrate the meaning systems of the pastoral action.

2. Is the person proposing to use the conceptual schema able to use it for understanding? This criterion for selecting a conceptual schema is so obvious that it can easily be overlooked. A given conceptual schema may be a thoroughly appropriate "match" for the action involved, but if the individual is unable to employ it in a manner that will enable penetration of the meaning of the action, the conceptual schema is not very helpful. Ricoeur says that texts are accessible to anyone who knows how to read. But Hirsch, following Piaget, implies that knowing how to read means having the conceptual capacities to understand what one is reading. The same is true for pastoral actions. Sometimes conceptual schemata are judged inadequate or inappropriate for understanding pastoral actions when in fact the problem was not the schema but the person using it. Technical knowledge of the schema is not enough. What is necessary is the capacity to use it in a making-matching, construction-correction process, in a fashion that permits reciprocity between the schema and the self-identity of the action.

3. Is the conceptual schema able to identify the world-disclosive possibilities of the action? This criterion follows from the first criterion that the conceptual schema needs to be able to help us penetrate the meanings of the action. But it goes on to specify that the conceptual schema should help us identify those meanings of the action that are world-disclosive. What does this mean in very practical terms? It means that the conceptual schema will help us understand not only "what happened" on a descriptive level, but also "what may be happening." In other words, what effects is the action having or likely to have that transcend its surface meanings? Is the action opening up possibilities for change or reorientation for those influ-

enced by it? The conceptual schema should enable us to determine whether the action has this world-disclosive potential.

Take, for example, the following pastoral action: Pastor Henry decides to refuse to marry a couple even though the parents of the prospective groom are influential members in her church. If she had simply gone ahead and married the couple, one doubts that the action would have had world-disclosive possibilities, at least of the magnitude that her refusal to marry them makes possible. In fact, had she gone ahead with the wedding, this action might not even qualify as "meaningful" action: "I married them, but my heart was not in it. It was just a ceremony as far as I was concerned." In contrast, her refusal to marry them is very likely to be meaningful. It will leave its mark (it will not go unnoticed as marrying the couple would have done). It will have unintended consequences (she may lose her job, the couple may thank her for refusing, and so forth). It will create a world to which those influenced by the action are led to reorient themselves (the couple may reconsider their intention to marry; the groom's parents may be prompted by this frustration of their expectations of the pastor to reconsider the meaning of the Christian life; and Pastor Henry may acquire a whole new under-standing of the power and vulnerability of the parish pastor). It will be open to reinterpretation ("Were there less drastic options avail-able to me? Did I do it because I was tired of being abused by Jerry's parents and not, as I originally claimed, because I had grave fears about the personal and moral maturity of this couple?" Or alterna-tively, Pastor Henry might discern later that her action reflected an even deeper respect for the couple than she was conscious of having at the time).

In selecting a conceptual schema, there should be a reasonable expectation that it will contribute to one's understanding of the action's world-disclosive possibilities. It should be able to illumine not just "what happened" (Pastor Henry's refusal to marry the couple) but also "what may be happening" (its possible effects in reorienting the lives of those influenced by it). This distinction between "what happened" and "what may be happening" is not based on temporal sequence, on what happened first and what happens later. Rather it is based on the distinction Ricoeur makes between the ostensive references of the text and meanings that are liberated from the text's ostensive references. This means that "what happened" and "what may be happening" can be simultaneous. It is simply that the one is on the surface of the action while the other stands in front of the action, projected outward from it. Or, put another way, "what happened" interprets the action while "what may be happening" interprets those who are influenced by the action.

4. Does the conceptual schema help us to *evaluate* the world-disclosive effects of the action? The conceptual schema should enable us not only to identify the action's world-disclosive effects, but also to make assessments of them. If Pastor Henry's refusal to marry the couple provides her with a new understanding of the power and vulnerability of the parish minister, and if it leads the couple to reconsider their relationship to one another, does the conceptual schema enable us to evaluate these reorientations to life?

Ethical or moral theories or models can be useful for evaluating pastoral actions. Pastor Henry could use such theories in determining whether the couple is ready for marriage.[2] Also, the conceptual schemata of psychologists and sociologists are rarely value-neutral. Thus they too may be useful for evaluating the effects of a pastoral action on those who have appropriated it in their lives.[3] Models derived from literary criticism may also be used to evaluate a given pastoral action because they often offer moral, aesthetic, and religious norms for assessing life-orientations. In chapter 4, I use a model derived from the study of autobiography for evaluating the world-disclosive effects of pastoral actions. Thus, various models (ethical, psychological, aesthetic) are available for evaluating pastoral actions, and may be incorporated into one's conceptual schema.

5. Does the conceptual schema help us place the pastoral action within the larger context of the pastor's praxis and pastoral self-understanding? One important way that a conceptual schema does this is by helping us understand the *intentionality* of the pastor in a given pastoral action. As we have seen, intentionality is to be distinguished from the pastor's conscious intention. It has less to do with what the pastors say they are attempting to do, and more with how they do it. We can make some initial guesses as to the intentionality involved in Pastor Henry's handling of the situation described above. But a conceptual schema would help us to penetrate beyond these initial guesses and enable us to identify the assumptions and expectations that inform how she goes about her pastoral work. As with texts, so with pastoral actions—these are tacit assumptions and expectations that may or may not be reflected in the pastor's conscious intentions. Also, like textual study, it is usually difficult to discern a pastor's intentionality on the basis of a single pastoral

action. Our confidence that we understand authors' intentionality increases as we gain access to more of their writings. This is also true of the pastoral actions of any given pastor. The more such actions we have access to, the more confident we become that we understand the intentionality involved.

Thus a conceptual schema is optimally useful if it enables us to view a given pastoral action against the background of the pastor's praxis and pastoral self-understanding. This is ultimately what literary critics seek to understand in their study of a given author. It is not enough that they penetrate the meaning of a single text. They also want to understand the author's praxis (three or four representative works if not the total corpus) and to gain insight into the author's self-understanding as an author. This does not ordinarily mean probing authors' personalities or investigating their private lives. What it does mean is gaining some understanding of what authors understand their work or vocation *as authors* to be. The same is true for understanding a pastor's praxis and pastoral self-understanding.

A CONCEPTUAL SCHEMA FOR
PASTORAL ACTION

By focusing on criteria for selecting a conceptual schema, I have already addressed questions of how they are employed and what we expect them to accomplish. But these questions can only be satisfactorily answered through a detailed example of a conceptual schema applicable to pastoral actions. The remaining pages of this chapter will be devoted to providing such an example. Then in chapter 4, I will apply this schema to a specific pastoral action.

The conceptual schema is based on my discussion of theological diagnosis in my book *Pastoral Counseling and Preaching.*[4] There I proposed that published sermons provide models of theological diagnosis useful for diagnostic efforts in pastoral care and counseling. Through content analysis of the published sermons of six well-known preachers, I was able to show that each preacher had a characteristic diagnostic approach, one that was common to most if not all of his published sermons. I then proposed that these six diagnostic approaches can be used for making theological diagnoses in pastoral care and counseling. In the original discussion of these six diagnostic approaches, I provided illustrative material from the sermons to support my descriptions of each approach. For our present purposes, I will simply identify the six types of theological diagnosis. Then I will reduce these six types to three diagnostic models, which then constitute the conceptual schema. Used this way, theology is not so much a normative science as an explanatory theory, useful for understanding the pastoral action in question.[5] Since these types were originally derived from preaching, they provide sufficient critical distance when applied to a case of pastoral visitation. The other four criteria are addressed by the schema itself.

SIX DIAGNOSTIC TYPES

1. *Theological diagnosis as identifying underlying personal motivations.* This diagnostic approach, employed by John Henry Newman, exposes the personal motives that are responsible for the problem being addressed by the sermon. Typical problems concern the absence of Christian love among Christ's people and the failure of Christians to combat evil. The preacher contends, however, that identifying these motives is difficult because we are largely unaware of them and we normally prefer a more superficial explanation. We do not like to accept the fact that the problem is due to some defect in our own motivational structure. The strength of this diagnostic approach is its attempt to bring unconscious motivations to consciousness, and its strong emphasis on insight as an initial step toward coming to terms with the problem. Its weakness is that sometimes the preacher imputes motives to persons that are irrelevant or even mistaken. Theologically, this diagnostic approach returns again and again to the judgment that our personal motives are often incompatible with the will of God, and the greatest challenge confronting Christians today is therefore to learn to conform their will to God's.

2. *Theological diagnosis as identifying the range of potential causes.* This diagnostic style, employed by John Wesley, explores the whole range of personal and situational factors that might cause the specific problem being addressed by the sermon. Typical problems concern spiritual dryness, the burdens of a sinful life, discouragement, and mental suffering. The preacher offers a veritable checklist from which listeners may select the most likely cause of their own particular difficulties with the problem. Among potential causes, the idea that God is responsible for the problem is regularly rejected, for God is understood to be working toward its resolution. The strength of this diagnostic approach is that it avoids simplistic explanations for problems, and instead recognizes their complexity. Its weakness is that it tends to view potential causes of the problem as all equally

serious. There is not much attempt to prioritize the causes in terms of their seriousness or severity. Theologically, this diagnostic approach focuses, in an almost relentless way, on the issue of responsibility. It asks, who or what is responsible for the problem? the individual? society? the work of unscrupulous individuals? or unavoidable circumstances of life?

3. *Theological diagnosis as exposing inadequate formulations of the problem.* This diagnostic approach, employed by Paul Tillich, exposes inadequate formulations of the problem in order to clear the way for a deeper understanding of it. Typical problems concern the difficulty of reconciling commitment to the Christian faith with modern consciousness, experiencing divine acceptance, and overcoming personal guilt. The preacher's diagnostic task is to encourage listeners to abandon superficial understandings and to risk opening themselves to its deeper meanings. Once these deeper meanings have been exposed, it is more difficult to think in terms of "resolving" the problem. More likely one will need to learn to live with its inherent ambiguity. The strength of this diagnostic approach is that it recommends abandoning the security of inadequate understandings of the problem and opening ourselves to its deeper meanings and complexities. It emphasizes the intrinsic value of exploring the depths of a problem, and not just trying to overcome the problem. Its weakness is that it challenges individuals to reject inadequate formulations of the problem when oftentimes these formulations, while perhaps ultimately inadequate, contain valuable truths and insights. The result is an all-or-nothing situation. The major theological issue addressed by this diagnostic approach is grace, which one discovers through relinquishing false securities and vain hopes: "My grace is sufficient for you."

4. *Theological diagnosis as discovering untapped personal and spiritual resources.* In this diagnostic approach employed by Phillips Brooks, the preacher points out that our problem would seem more manageable if we would recognize our vast store of personal and spiritual resources. Typical problems addressed in these sermons include the loss of the visions of one's youth, and inability to cope with a besetting sin or malady such as alcoholism, personal discouragement, or profound loneliness. In each case the preacher challenges his listeners to view these problems in light of their previous experience. Did they not find the personal and spiritual strength to overcome similar problems in the past? Is not this strength available to them now? The power of this diagnostic style is the fact that it is right; many prob-

lems are manageable when we utilize the personal and spiritual resources that are available to us. The weakness of this style is the danger that it will replace careful diagnosis of the problem with vague optimism. Also, some problems are more intractable than others, and some of these intractable problems have no solution this side of the grave. The theological issue that this diagnostic approach continually addresses is the dual theme of memory and hope. The preacher encourages his listeners to remember God's faithfulness in the past and to live in hope of God's faithfulness in the future.

5. *Theological diagnosis as bringing clarity to the problem.* In this diagnostic approach, employed by Austin Farrar, the preacher contends that the major reason we have difficulty with a problem is that we have not yet gotten it clarified. This applies to such problems as the conflict between religion and science, the problem of suffering and evil, and the difficult moral dilemmas confronting Christians in every age. The preacher suggests that as long as our understanding of the problem remains confused and befuddled, we will not be able to do much about it. But the preacher insists that the fundamental problems of Christian faith can be rendered clear and transparent if we have the intellectual and moral courage to address them. The strength of this diagnostic style is that problems are not considered inherently enigmatical; we simply lack the will or energy to clarify them. Its potential danger is that the goal of clarification can lead to simplification; sometimes a sermon using this diagnostic approach makes the problem appear simpler than it really is. The theological issue that this diagnostic approach addresses most consistently is the matter of truth: God is truth, and God is on the side of truth against error and deception. The search for truth is therefore not an intellectual luxury but a religious and moral obligation placed on those who claim to be seekers after God.

6. *Theological diagnosis that assesses a problem in terms of the deepest intentions of shared human experience.* In this diagnostic approach, employed by Friedrich Schleiermacher, the problem under review is understood in light of our deepest human intentions or capacities, such as love, fidelity, courage, and compassion. Typical problems addressed are family relations, the community's response to the destructive effects of war and epidemics, and the death of a child. This diagnostic approach assumes a deep and basic congruity between the Christian faith and humanity's deepest capacities for sharing one another's burdens and joys. The obvious strength of this

diagnostic style is that it places strong emphasis on the social and communal dimensions of human life, and encourages intentions of love, fidelity and other basic virtues. Its potential weakness is that the assessment of the problem can be rather subjective, focused so heavily on human intentions that the objective reality of the problem is in danger of being overlooked. It contrasts in this regard with diagnostic approach 2 (identifying the range of potential causes of the problem), which is much more concerned with the problem as an objective reality. The central theological theme in this diagnostic style is love, for God's love is viewed as the deepest divine intention, and human intentions are evaluated for the degree to which they reflect such love.

THREE DIAGNOSTIC MODALITIES

These six diagnostic approaches are the basic ingredients of the conceptual schema I wish to apply to a pastoral action (in chapter 4). But they have not yet been formulated into such a schema. The next step is to take these six diagnostic approaches and locate them on three axes, with each axis viewed as a *model* of theological diagnosis. I will call these the *contextual, experiential,* and *revisionist* models of theological diagnosis.

The *contextual model* includes these two diagnostic approaches: identifying potential causes of the problem (Wesley) and identifying untapped personal and spiritual resources for dealing with the problem (Brooks). I call it contextual because it is primarily concerned to place the problem in a meaningful context so that it may be dealt with more effectively. I think of this as the "look around you" model of diagnosis, with the first approach (Wesley) encouraging us to look for the potential causes of the problem and the second (Brooks) encouraging us to look for the resources that are available to deal with it. It tends to take a rather hopeful view overall, based on the conviction that for every cause there is an available resource for dealing with it. God is on the side of coping, hope, and eventual victory.

The *experiential* model includes these two diagnostic approaches: exposing inadequate formulations of the problem (Tillich) and viewing the problem in light of our capacity for deeply shared experience (Schleiermacher). I call it experiential because it takes the view that problems need to be understood in terms of how we experience them. If the previous model encourages us to "look around you," this model encourages us to "look more deeply into ourselves and others." Discerning how we and they experience problems is more important than looking to the causes of problems and to our resources for dealing with them. The first diagnostic approach in this model (Tillich) sees the problem as the occasion for deeper self-understanding while the second diagnostic approach (Schleiermacher) draws our attention to what is profoundly human in all of us. Together, they invite us to engage our deeper selves and the deeper selves of others. They recognize that even though such engagement is often more painful than satisfying for ourselves and others, it ultimately results in the even deeper experience of the grace and love of God.

The *revisionist model* includes the two remaining diagnostic styles: identifying underlying personal motivations (Newman) and bringing new clarity to the problem (Farrar). I call this the revisionist model because it takes the view that our problems need to be looked at in a new way. The reason we do not see them clearly or accurately is that we are looking at them in ways that allow them to remain opaque. If the contextual model encourages looking around us, and the experiential model encourages looking more deeply into ourselves and others, this model encourages looking from a new perspective. The first of these two diagnostic approaches (Newman) says that the underlying source of the problem is not what we have perceived it to be, while the second (Farrar) says that our angle of vision on the problem is wrong. Both agree that the problem needs ultimately to be viewed from God's angle of vision. This new perspective may be humbling and chastening because our sins and stupidity are thereby brought to light, but it overcomes deception and illusion, and the goal of the Christian life is to leave deception and follow after truth.

In chapter 4, I will discuss a pastoral action in which the pastor used of one of these models. However, to illustrate how all three models might function in a given pastoral care situation, I would like to consider briefly the following case from Cryer and Vayhinger's *Casebook in Pastoral Counseling.*[6] This case is similar to the case I will be discussing later because both concern the pastoral care of aging persons.

The situation is this: Mildred is a member of Pastor Larson's church; her husband Tom is not. Mildred and Tom have a son nineteen and a daughter sixteen. Two years ago Tom's mother died, and since then his seventy-two-year-old father has been living with Mildred and Tom. As Mildred describes "Grandpa," he is selfish, overbearing, and filthy in his personal habits. He intrudes on Mildred's privacy, exposes himself less than half-clothed to his granddaughter, opens and reads Mildred's personal letters, and nags at a little girl Mildred keeps during the day to supplement the family income. He meets people at the door and often dismisses them, even when Mildred is expecting them. He receives a modest old-age pension, none of which he contributes to his support.

Mildred came to the pastor one day because "I've done something awful—I slapped Grandpa!" In the course of the pastoral conversation (which took place at the pastor's home with his wife present), it was revealed that there had been a similar crisis before (though not involving actual physical violence), and Grandpa had gone to live with his nephew. But "he wasn't satisfied, and Tom had to go and get him." Pastor Larson's wife suggested that Mildred might get a job outside the home so as not to have to be around Grandpa during the day when Tom was not home, but Mildred expressed fear that Grandpa, with his penchant for leaving his cigars around the house, might "burn the house down." Pastor Larson felt this was a chance worth taking, and Mildred herself proposed that she might take care of the little girl in the girl's own home. But Mildred kept returning to the problem of her "hatred" for Grandpa, which prompted Pastor Larson to focus on what this whole problem with Grandpa might be doing to Mildred's faith. He first affirmed Mildred ("I know you too well, Mildred, to think for a moment that you are going to let this thing destroy you or get you down") and then acknowledged that Mildred has "a real problem," but when it is solved "your faith will be as strong as ever, even stronger." He suggested that Mildred talk to Tom and tell him she is sorry for having slapped Grandpa, and then arrange for a family council with the pastor present in which everyone "lays their cards on the table." In the pastor's judgment, the result would be that Tom would see Mildred's side of the story and would agree that "the only way to avoid complete wreckage of your home is to get Grandpa in a home for the aged."

The family council with the pastor present did not take place. Instead, Mildred discussed the problem with Tom, and Tom said to her, "I want to see the preacher. We're going to get this thing settled right. Honey, I can't live without you!" That evening Tom came to see Pastor Larson and came to the decision to put his father in a home. The pastor then encouraged Tom to think about his own "spiritual state," pointing out that "he would find spiritual strength the greatest help he could have in meeting this difficult problem."

Tom said he would give this suggestion serious consideration and then left. Acting on Tom's advice, Mildred left the next day for a rest and a visit with out-of-state relatives. A few days later Pastor and Mrs. Larson received a letter from Mildred indicating that "I do not really hate Grandpa" and that sometimes she thinks she could go back and "live above it all" (i.e., not let Grandpa's presence distress her so) but "I do not completely trust this attitude."

Our concern here is not to provide a complete analysis and evaluation of this case, but simply to illustrate how a contextualist, experientialist, and revisionist might address this case in quite different ways. First, the contextualist. The contextualist would focus on the whole range of issues that are causing the problem, and on the various resources available for dealing with it. Among the causes considered, we would expect the contextualist to emphasize the effect of Grandpa's changed circumstances (his wife's death and the loss of his own home) on his current behavior. He acts as though Tom and Mildred's home is his own. We would also expect the contextualist to put Mildred's "hatred" for Grandpa in context (i.e., he is *Tom's* father, not hers; he is not expected to make a financial contribution to the family; he deprives Mildred of her privacy and flouts her Christian values, as when he exposes himself to her daughter). Among the available resources, Pastor Larson focused on two: the nursing home for Grandpa, and Mildred's spiritual resources. The possibility of Mildred getting out of the house during the day was also considered but then was unaccountably dropped as a possible resource. A more thoroughgoing contextualist would have considered other resources, such as a contractual arrangement with Grandpa's nephew to share the burden of caring for Grandpa on an alternating basis; ways to get Grandpa out of the house during the day (e.g., volunteer work at the church, involvement in a senior citizens' center); other care facilities for Grandpa that would be less extreme than the nursing home option; and various other resources the family has available to it but have not been brought to bear on the problem (e.g., helpful involvement by Tom and Mildred's teenage children, or other thus far unmentioned resources that Grandpa himself has available to him). These additional resources might well have come out in the open if the pastor's family council idea had materialized. As it happened, the problem was "solved" without Grandpa's or the children's own input. To the contextualist, it was solved too easily, and the fact that other resources were not considered will undoubtedly come back to haunt both Mildred and Tom.

Second, the experientialist. The experientialist would focus on how Mildred, Tom, Grandpa, and the children are experiencing the whole situation, with the hope that all would begin to experience it as a shared problem, not the problem of separate individuals. This approach would focus on emotions. How does Tom feel about the conflict between his wife and his father? Does he feel that he is being forced to choose between loyalty to his wife and to his father? What are Grandpa's feelings in the situation? Is he still grieving over his wife's death? Does he resent having lost his independence? Is he angry at Mildred for slapping him? How do the children feel about the situation, especially the daughter to whom Grandpa has exposed himself? We *do* know a great deal about how Mildred is experiencing this problem, though the conflictful nature of her feelings becomes more self-evident in her letter to the pastor and his wife after the problem itself has been "resolved." Now it becomes evident that her feelings toward Grandpa are mixed. No, "I do not really hate Grandpa. . . ." Had an experientialist met with the family in the proposed family council, much attention would have been given to the emotions felt toward one another, painful as it may be for them to reveal these emotions to each other. One senses that the most difficult revelations would not be between Mildred and Grandpa, but between Mildred and Tom. "Why did Tom allow me to be put in this impossible situation?" "Why can't Mildred get along better with my father?"

The experientialist would allow the "resolution" of the problem to emerge from this exploration of their emotions, and would hope that whatever decisions are made would grow out of the family members' sense that the problem is a shared problem for which all have responsibility. The experientialist would not be so quick to propose "solutions," such as Mildred working outside the home or Grandpa being put in a home, because these are solutions that are essentially based on environmental changes, whereas the experientialist seeks changes on the interpersonal level and anticipates that this can only occur when the family members begin to open their hearts to one another.

Third, the revisionist. The revisionist would place emphasis on the realization of new perspectives on the situation, and new and more accurate perceptions of one another. The revisionist might agree, for example, with Mildred's perception of Grandpa as selfish and filthy, but would also encourage her to perceive that his tendency to be "overbearing" and controlling of the situation may mask a sense that he is losing control of his life. And what is the meaning of his desire to expose himself, on the one hand, and his refusal to allow Mildred any privacy, on the other? Does this theme of exposure/ privacy tell us something important about him? Then, there is Mildred's own self-perception. She presents herself as frustrated by Grandpa, and is conscious of the fact that her frustrations are undermining her perception of herself as a good Christian. Pastor Larson here has an opportunity to challenge her perception of what it means to be a good Christian, but he tends to buy into it himself when he suggests that her faith journey is somehow separate from the problem at hand, as though this problem is mainly an unfortunate distracting episode in her otherwise steady spiritual growth. The revisionist would encourage her, instead, to view this very problem as an opportunity to restructure her perceptions of what it means to be a Christian self. This would first involve gaining a more accurate picture of herself, especially in her relations with Grandpa and Tom. She presents herself as *frustrated* by Grandpa's demeanor. The revisionist would accept this self-perception, but would also note that she is *mixed up* about Grandpa (as she confesses in her letter). Similarly, she finds Tom's *openness* to resolving the problem surprising and refreshing, and yet seems to *suspect* it, because Tom is doing it because he does not want to lose her. Surely she must wonder what price she will have to pay in the future for gaining Tom's support now. These various aspects of herself (frustrated, mixed-up, surprised, suspicious) add up to a very complex self-understanding. The revisionist would want to resist the simplistic self-perception reflected in her perception of herself as a "good Christian," and would take advantage of the recent assault on this self-perception (i.e., by slapping Grandpa she also injured this self-perception) to bring to light her more complex self.

One important aspect of this approach would be to encourage her to do more of the kind of self-reflection she does in her letter, where she acknowledges that the situation involving Grandpa has made her very uncertain about herself. Who, after all, is the real Mildred? The one who is so frustrated by Grandpa that she is driven to slapping him? Or the one who believes she may be able to "live above it all"? Is she the frustrated wife who tells her husband he must choose between loyalty to her or to his father? Or is she the self-assured woman who senses that she has the inner strength to cope with Grandpa and, in the process, to help *him* become a more responsible man? Certainly she is a mixture of both, but the actual resolution of the problem deprived her of the opportunity to develop the latter dimension of herself. In the interests of preserving her faith she was denied the opportunity to begin looking at herself in a new way. Slapping Grandpa remains an "awful" thing to have done, rather than the first decisive act in a continuing process of self-emancipation.

In short, the revisionist would focus on Mildred's perceptions of Grandpa, Tom, and especially herself, and would seek to determine whether they are credible and whether they are capable of change. Like the experientialist, the revisionist would not suggest a change in the family living arrangements until these perceptions had been given careful scrutiny. But the revisionist would place greater emphasis than the experientialist on *perceptual* change, and how such perceptual change actually changes the situation itself. This does not mean that Mildred need simply view her relations with Grandpa in a more positive light and agree to try to make the best of the situation by perceiving it differently. In fact, she may come to the opposite view, that is, that her willingness to suffer under Grandpa's overbearing ways has in fact deprived him of opportunities to become a more responsible person. Or she may conclude that among her many strengths (both spiritual and personal) she lacks the inner strength to cope with Grandpa and, moreover, does not believe she has to apologize for this "lack" to any man, including Tom, Pastor Larson, Grandpa, or God himself. In this case, the ultimate resolution of the problem may be very similar to what the contextualist approach devises, but it is based on consideration of Mildred's self-perception, not on Mildred as one among various available resources. Finally, note that the revisionist is much less concerned than either the contextualist or the experientialist to involve the whole family in the counseling process. The spotlight is directed toward Mildred, and it is ultimately not Grandpa but Mildred herself who is "exposed" to its piercing rays.

We could discuss these three diagnostic models in greater detail, but I believe that enough has been said about them to enable us to differentiate one from another. Also, now that the six diagnostic approaches have been organized according to three diagnostic models, we have a conceptual schema that is manageable enough to use for understanding pastoral actions. Yet, at the same time, it is general enough for use with many different forms of pastoral actions. The case that I will use in chapter 4 to illustrate this conceptual schema in depth happens to involve hospital visitation, but there is no reason why the schema could not be used for understanding other forms of pastoral care. The limiting factor here is not the form of pastoral action but the fact that the conceptual schema tends to be problem oriented, and may therefore be most useful for understanding pastoral care actions that are concerned with problems.

What do we expect these diagnostic models to contribute to our understanding of a given pastoral action? First, we expect that they would help us to understand "what happened" in the action, that is, that they would be useful for getting at the ostensive references of the action. Second, they should enable us to understand "what may be happening," to identify the world-disclosive possibilities of the action. Third, these models should enable us to evaluate the action's world-disclosive effects on the persons involved. Fourth, use of these models should help us to see this action in the larger context of the pastor's praxis and pastoral self-understanding.

As formulated thus far, our conceptual schema should permit us to clarify the ostensive meaning of the action (1) and identify its world-disclosive possibilities (2). However, it has not yet been sufficiently developed to enable us to *evaluate* the world-disclosive possibilities of the action (3) or to place this action in the larger context of the pastor's praxis and pastoral self-understanding (4). The following discussion expands the schema to include pastoral praxis and self-understanding (4). The issue of evaluation (3) will be deferred to chapter 4.

THREE PASTORAL MODALITIES

The pastoral models of shepherd, wounded healer, and wise fool are meant to address the issue of pastoral praxis and self-understanding. The implicit assumption behind each of these models is that the pastor does not engage in discrete pastoral actions having no continuity with one another, but that the pastor's actions (praxis) fit more or less together as an integral whole. And what accounts for this consistency? Alastair Campbell's view that the pastor's personal character has much to do with it may have considerable merit. But our hermeneutical model suggests that one's *pastoral self-understanding* is a more important factor. The images of shepherd, wounded healer, and wise fool, all discussed in Campbell's *Rediscovering Pastoral Care*, reflect three distinctive pastoral self-understandings that are capable of integrating one's praxis. Some pastors feel that their pastoral work ought not to be informed by a single model but a multiplicity of models. They argue for a kind of creative eclecticism. Other pastors say that their work is not informed by any pastoral self-understanding, that they simply do whatever needs to be done. The pastoral theologians who developed these models would support the former claim, as long as the pastor is aware that *creative* eclectics are intentional about how they go about fusing two or more pastoral modalities. They would, however, reject the latter claim, contending that a pastor's praxis is always informed by some pastoral self-understanding. They would say that such models help us become more conscious of how our pastoral self-understanding informs our praxis, and more conscious of the fact that differences in the way pastors approach problems and needs are not merely differences in style but in pastoral self-understanding.

At the risk of some oversimplification, I suggest that the three pastoral images of shepherd, wounded healer, and wise fool fit my three models of theological diagnosis. The shepherd fits the contextual model. The wounded healer fits the experiential model. And the wise fool fits the revisionist model. Through these linkages, our conceptual schema is expanded to include the issues of praxis and pastoral self-understanding. Let us consider the rationale for connecting these pastoral images to their respective diagnostic models as indicated in Figure A.

The shepherd and the contextual type. In the biblical setting, the shepherd is one who knows the world in which the sheep live and understands its peril and places of safety and nourishment. The shepherd does not attempt to shield the sheep from every difficulty the world puts before them, but the shepherd does help the sheep to cope with these difficulties by his or her guiding presence and solicitous gestures. The shepherd is conscious of the limit situations confronting the sheep, especially death and other serious threats to the sheep's well-being.

The shepherd's own self-understanding focuses on the role of helpful guidance. The shepherd is one who, as Hiltner puts it, does his or her work with an "attitude of tender and solicitous concern."[7] The shepherd does not, however, allow his or her guidance to become coercive or paternalistic. As Hiltner also says, the ultimate purpose of pastoral care is to help people help themselves.[8] The shepherd guides but does not deprive the sheep of their freedom to act for themselves, even if this means making mistakes they will later

FIGURE A
A CONCEPTUAL SCHEMA FOR INTERPRETING PASTORAL ACTIONS

DIAGNOSTIC MODELS	PASTORAL MODELS
Contextual Model	*Shepherd*
Approach to Problem:	Praxis:
1) *causes* of problem	1) views problem in *context*
2) available *resources*	2) identifies relevant *resources*
Anticipated Disclosure:	Self-Understanding:
resourceful God justifying hope	ministry of competent guidance
Experiential Model	*Wounded Healer*
Approach to Problem:	Praxis:
1) how problem is *experienced*	1) shares the *pain* of others
2) how problem may be *shared*	2) encourages deeper *experience* of self and others
Anticipated Disclosure:	Self-Understanding: ministry
graceful God supporting *risk* and loving God sharing *pain*	of personal vulnerability
Revisionist Model	*Wise Fool*
Approach to Problem:	Praxis:
1) see *problem* in new way	1) challenges *distortions*
2) see *ourselves* in new way	2) encourages new *perspectives*
Anticipated Disclosure:	Self-Understanding:
perceptive God evoking *truth*	ministry of basic truthfulness

regret. This image of the shepherd, while having obvious roots in the Old Testament ("The Lord is my shepherd"), is also associated with Jesus, who is described in the gospels as the shepherd whose concern for the sheep was so great that he laid down his life so that they might be spared. He is also described as the one whose absence led sheep to scatter. Without the shepherd they lost all sense of meaningful context.

This image of the shepherd fits our contextual model because the shepherd is aware of the *range* of possible causes of the sheep's discomfort, and of the various *resources* available to the sheep for coping with the perils of life. The shepherd knows the context in which the sheep live, and this means being aware not only of its potential threats and snares, but also its places of refuge and peace. Furthermore, the shepherd's ministry reflects a spirit of hope and confidence: "Even though I walk through the valley of the shadow of death, I fear no evil; for thou art with me; thy rod and thy staff, they comfort me" (Ps. 23:4).

The wounded healer and the experiential type. Like the shepherd image, the wounded healer has a biblical foundation. It is most clearly based on the image of the suffering Christ. Campbell describes the wounded healer as the one who

> restores the fractured relationships between God, humanity, and the whole universe. . . . Jesus' wounds, in life and death, are the expressions of his openness to our suffering. He suffered because of his love: his sufferings are the stigmata of his care for us and for the whole world estranged from God.[9]

Here Campbell suggests that the sufferings of Christ promote healing because they are the consequence of his deep love for us, and such love heals: "Such wounded love has a healing power because it is enfleshed love, entering into human weakness, feeling our pain, standing beside us in our dereliction."[10] In the same way, the pastor as wounded healer is motivated by love and not for purposes of self-promotion. In suffering for others, the pastor participates in our common humanity. It is true, as Campbell points out, that "we can never fully enter into the pain of another person, whether or not we have experienced something similar in our own lives."[11] Everyone's suffering is unique. But "at the same time we are not so different in our experiences that no communication, no reverberation of feeling is possible."[12] Thus, on some deep level, pain is sharable and we can know and understand the sufferings of another.

The ultimate intention of the wounded healer is to see that suffering gives way to healing. But the wounded healer model says that healing comes not by distancing ourselves from painful experience, or even "working through" our pain, but by living our pain, allowing ourselves to experience it fully. As Nouwen says in *The Wounded Healer:* "A minister is not a doctor whose primary task is to take away pain. Rather he deepens the pain to a level where it can be shared."[13] This means rejecting the false supposition that life should be painless, free from fear, despair, loneliness, and estrangement. Indeed, those who avoid life's pain are ultimately the poorer for it, because as we live our pain fully we also experience the unremitting love of God and the peace that passes all understanding.

The wounded healer image fits our *experiential* model because this model stresses the importance of experiencing deeply. It recognizes that the deeper we go into our experience the more we experience our common humanity with others. It also emphasizes that as we engage our deeper selves, we acquire an even deeper awareness of the love of God. The wounded healer image recognizes that the problems we confront in life are the occasion for deeper self-understanding. It also recognizes that as we penetrate the deepest levels of our self-understanding, we discover not what makes us unique as persons but what we have in common with other selves. The wounded healer has the same concern for the suffering of others that we saw in the shepherd but does not address this concern by seeking to mobilize the available resources for alleviating pain. Rather, the wounded healer encourages us to live our pain as deeply as we are able, to drink the bitter cup down to its very dregs. While the shepherd holds out hope to those whose well-being has been threatened, promising that relief will surely come, the wounded healer stresses that whatever may happen, we will know the power of God's love. Both envision victory over the powers of sickness and death, but the shepherd emphasizes our hope in God's deliverance while the wounded healer stresses the abiding presence of God whose love knows no limits: "If I go to the depths of hell, thou art there."

The wise fool and the revisionist type. The "wise fool" is Campbell's term for an image of the pastor initially proposed by Heije Faber, who suggested that the hospital chaplain functions much like the clown in a circus.[14] Campbell suggests that the wise fool, like the previous two images, has biblical roots. He cites Paul's advice to the Christian community in Corinth: "If anyone among you thinks he is wise by this world's standards, he should become a fool, in order to be really wise" (1 Cor. 3:18). On this basis, the pastor is neither worldly wise nor "just a fool," but an apparent fool who is in fact a person of wisdom. Campbell suggests that the major characteristics of the wise fool are *simplicity* (reflected in a refreshing directness and refusal to put on personal airs or engage in professional gamesmanship); *loyalty* (reflected in an undramatic but persistent loyalty to others in disregard of self); and *prophecy* (reflected in a tendency to challenge the accepted norms, conventions, and authorities within the society). Pastors who adopt this self-understanding risk being thought unorthodox by their peers in the profession, but they may also command their peers' respect for daring to challenge the empty professionalism and self-promotion in much contemporary ministry. Pastors who adopt this self-understanding are also frequently underestimated or taken for granted. Others may fail to see that these "fools" are actually wise, and may therefore dismiss their proposals and insights as unrealistic or unworthy of serious consideration.

The major function of the wise fool is to help us "to see ourselves in a clearer light."[15] This function is perhaps most dramatically evident when the wise fool is being prophetic, but it is no less present in the wise fool's simplicity and loyalty. Through prophecy, the wise fool challenges us to see what our social institutions are doing to us. Through personal simplicity, the wise fool challenges us to conduct our professional lives with less self-serving distortion. Through personal loyalty, the wise fool challenges us to be more truthful in our interpersonal relationships.

In challenging us to see ourselves in a clearer light, the pastoral image of the wise fool fits our *revisionist model*. As we have seen, this model emphasizes our need to view life's situations in new ways. It suggests that we are not seeing our problems clearly because we have preferred darkness and deception to light and truth. The wise fool challenges this preference for darkness and deception, inviting us to view our situation from God's perspective. If we could view our problems more consistently from this perspective we would recognize that they are not as complex as they may seem. Truth is remarkably simple; error is unnecessarily complex. Professional and personal relationships can be remarkably clear and straightforward if we do not insist on deceiving one another, but instead relate to each other with the same honesty and straightforwardness with which God relates to us. In effect, the wise fool exemplifies the revisionist model by reversing our customary ways of perceiving the world and other selves (including God, the Ultimate Self). What we formerly considered foolishness is now wisdom, and our former wisdom is now folly. Such reversals reveal a new world to us, one to which we had previously been blind or impervious.

These linkages between pastoral images and our diagnostic models may not be perfect in every respect, but they are certainly close enough to justify incorporating these pastoral modalities into our conceptual schema, providing us a means of viewing a pastoral action within the larger context of the pastor's ongoing praxis and pastoral self-understanding.

We are now ready to apply our schema to the pastoral action

selected for this illustration. My hope is that the diagnostic models will enable us to clarify the ostensive meaning of the action ("what happened") and also identify the world-disclosive possibilities of the action ("what may be happening"). We should, however, be prepared for the possibility that one of these diagnostic models will prove more valuable than the others. We would also hope that the pastoral images will help us place the action in the context of the pastor's praxis and pastoral self-understanding. It may turn out that the action is informed by either the shepherd, wounded healer, or wise fool image. If so, perhaps we will be able to discern whether or not the pastor in this case is using this image with clear intentionality to inform his pastoral self-understanding.

CHAPTER 4

A Case of
Pastoral Intervention

Elizabeth is a ninety-two-year-old blind woman in Pastor Dugan's congregation. A few months before the pastoral action to be reported on here, she quit attending church. Previously, she was brought to church by the church custodian, but refused to come anymore after an incident of theft at her home. Her son had died two years earlier but she kept his car parked in the front yard of her house. One evening the tires on the car were stolen and she accused Tom, the church custodian, of the theft. Pastor Dugan tried to convince Elizabeth that her charges were groundless, but she would not listen to him, and instead quit attending church because she no longer trusted the custodian.

As the theft of the tires indicates, Elizabeth's house is in a neighborhood with a reputation for burglary. Since her son's death, she has lived in the house alone. Twice in the last eight years her house has been damaged by fire. The house is dirty, cluttered, and in bad repair. Elizabeth has been encouraged by her social service aide and various neighbors to move elsewhere, but adamantly refuses. She sits in one specific chair through the day and often through the night. She does not eat well and resists seeing the doctor for her skin infections. However, she is quite lucid and generally healthy except for her occasional sores, swollen legs, and, of course, her blindness. She rejects the idea that she belongs in a hospital and has no interest whatsoever in going to a nursing home.

The pastoral action that concerns us here was precipitated by the following event. One night, Elizabeth apparently became disoriented and wandered out of the house into the street. She was rescued by a neighbor, who reported the incident to Elizabeth's social service aide. The aide took her to a psychiatric hospital. She was admitted to the hospital on the grounds that she suffered from hallucinations. Once in the hospital, she was tested for mental disorders. Although nothing was found, the hospital staff refused to release her because they did not want to accept responsibility for allowing her to go home without round-the-clock supervision. Anticipating that she would never be released, the hospital, through its social service officer, asked Pastor Dugan, in lieu of family, to form a committee of church people to manage her financial affairs. Pastor Dugan was not unwilling to help in this regard, but he also knew that if he or the church accepted legal responsibility for Elizabeth's affairs, they would be going along with the hospital's intentions to keep her indefinitely. At first, he accepted the idea that Elizabeth should not be allowed to return home and began to lay the groundwork for the church's eventual legal guardianship. But after a number of pastoral visits with Elizabeth during which she pleaded with him to get her released from the hospital, he began to reconsider.

Following one conversation in which Elizabeth raised suspicions that the social service aide had taken advantage of her by having her admitted to the hospital, Pastor Dugan began to doubt the wisdom of his compliance with the hospital social worker's plans. He felt that the aide did in fact maneuver Elizabeth into the psychiatric hospital by alleging that she suffered from hallucinations. He began to ask himself, "What right does anyone have to remove someone from her home against her will?" He decided to ask the hospital social worker to secure legal representation for Elizabeth from the hospital legal staff, on the grounds that Elizabeth was at least entitled to a court hearing, and that the hospital was obligated to provide legal counsel. The social worker acceded to his request and she began to work out the arrangements for the hearing. Pastor Dugan confesses that he did not have much hope that the court hearing would result in Elizabeth's release, but felt it would help her to know that everything possible was done to respond to her desires. He felt this might contribute to a more positive adjustment to the hospital.

However, before the court hearing took place, Pastor Dugan had what he calls an "unsettling experience." He had gone to the hospital to see Elizabeth. But when he entered the visitors' room, a Mrs. Parker was sitting there waiting to see him. She explained to Pastor Dugan that her role, as a blind person herself, was to help blind patients adjust to hospital life. She asked Pastor Dugan to intervene

with Elizabeth to convince her to receive Mrs. Parker and her services. But Pastor Dugan politely refused, telling her that Elizabeth
was totally closed to the idea of remaining in the hospital. However,
he suggested that should the judge in the pending court hearing
decide that Elizabeth would remain in the hospital, perhaps she
would then be more receptive to Mrs. Parker's services. This ended
their conversation and shortly thereafter Elizabeth was brought into
the visitors' room. Elizabeth informed Pastor Dugan that the court
hearing had originally been scheduled for that very morning but
that it was subsequently canceled, and she did not know why. Pastor
Dugan acknowledged that he knew nothing about the originally
scheduled hearing nor why it was abruptly canceled, but told
Elizabeth he would investigate. Elizabeth reiterated her determination to get out of the hospital and asked Pastor Dugan to help her. As
she put it, "I am not sick like the others here." Pastor Dugan agreed,
but asked her why she wandered out of the house that night. Was she
suffering from hallucinations? She said she could not remember the
incident at all.

As they were talking, Mrs. Parker returned with the ward psychiatrist. Dr. Blessing, the psychiatrist, began to quiz Elizabeth concerning her refusal to cooperate with Mrs. Parker. Pastor Dugan later
observed, not without some anger, "He preempted my conversation
with Elizabeth." Then the psychiatrist told Elizabeth that she would
definitely not be going home and that he had personally called
off the court hearing because it was pointless. Pastor Dugan was
stunned by this, and requested to see Dr. Blessing in his office
after concluding his pastoral visit with Elizabeth. Shortly thereafter he went to Dr. Blessing's office and explained that he was not
trying to undermine the hospital's care of Elizabeth, but felt she
needed a "sense of closure" in order to adjust to the hospital, and
this meant having the court hearing. Dr. Blessing replied that he
had tried to talk the lawyer out of doing anything about the case
because "the judge would laugh him out of court." Thoroughly dis-
satisfied with this explanation, Pastor Dugan stood his ground and
said he would continue to work for the court hearing.

He left the doctor's office feeling very angry—angry at the doctor
"who seemed to parade his power at the expense of people helpless
before it," but also angry at Elizabeth. He recalled how she turned
against the church's custodian even though Tom had given gener-
ously of his time for her, and he sensed that his own efforts in her
behalf would undoubtedly win the same "appreciation." He found

himself muttering, "Old woman, if you weren't so selfish, we wouldn't be in this mess." But the following day he called the lawyer assigned to Elizabeth's case. The lawyer agreed to seek another court hearing date, and to inform Pastor Dugan when it was scheduled.

The day of the hearing came and Pastor Dugan testified in behalf of Elizabeth and her desire to return home. He did so not without some misgivings, recalling that her house had been nearly destroyed by fire on two occasions, and still wondering what had prompted Elizabeth to walk out into the street that night. Dr. Blessing also testified, arguing that Elizabeth was incompetent to live at home and that the hospital would be contributing to her almost certain death if it released her. But the testimony that weighed most heavily with the judge was Elizabeth's own. Addressing him as "pastor,"she told the judge how she had prayed to Almighty God to be allowed to return home, to spend her last days there in contentment and peace. Listening to her appeal, Pastor Dugan sensed that Elizabeth had carefully prepared both mentally and spiritually for this hour, that her every word and gesture were carefully chosen to convince the judge that she was competent to return home. She was fighting for her independence and, as Pastor Dugan says, it was a "fine performance."

After hearing these testimonies, the judge ordered her release from the hospital and said she was to be returned home. He lectured Dr. Blessing: "If it were our job to protect every old person from all potential dangers, they would all be institutionalized." And he also complimented Pastor Dugan: "It's obvious this woman has a friend in you and the church." Pastor Dugan appreciated the compliment, but also worried that the church's obligations to Elizabeth would increase with her return home. Still, he had scored a victory, one greater than he had expected. His goal had been to see that Elizabeth's rights to a court hearing were honored so that she might have a "sense of closure" about the manner in which she was hospitalized. He did not really expect that she would gain her release. Yet, it was a victory that was not without a price, for he was understandably anxious about what it portended for Elizabeth, for him, and for the congregation.

A MEANINGFUL ACTION

Before we bring our conceptual schema into the picture, we should establish that this pastoral action fits the characteristics of meaningful action. This is not very difficult to do.

First, Pastor Dugan's intervention in Elizabeth's behalf "leaves its mark" because it clearly had significance beyond the moment. It would have a lasting effect on Elizabeth's future.

Second, this pastoral action also had unintended consequences. Pastor Dugan's conscious intention was for Elizabeth to have her day in court so that she would adjust better to her institutionalization. That the hearing resulted in her release from the hospital was an unintended consequence of his action.

Third, this pastoral action "created a world" that transcended the situation itself. The court hearing especially disclosed a world of meaning that was larger than the immediate situation. Both Pastor Dugan and Dr. Blessing had miscalculated what would happen in the court hearing, and both became witnesses of an event that transcended the considerations of professional prerogative and expertise that had defined the whole matter to that point. All of this was preempted as a judge and an old woman confronted one another. What happened next was a world-disclosure we have encountered before in Jesus' parable of the judge and the importunate widow (Luke 18:1–8). Elizabeth's judge had a more kindly disposition than the judge in the parable, but the two stories disclose essentially the same world. Both judges gave the woman her "just rights." Both did so because the women appealed so strongly, and both did so even though they would have been "justified" had they decided against the women. But most important, neither acted like judges. Pastor Dugan and Dr. Blessing came to the hearing expecting the judge to act like a "judge" and treat Elizabeth accordingly. Elizabeth came hoping that he would not act like a "judge." She "mistakenly" called him a "pastor" and informed him that she had been praying to Almighty God for her release. This "mistake" suggested that she wanted him to relinquish his "judge" role in favor of a more "pastoral" role. And, indeed, he was not the "judge" that Pastor Dugan and certainly Dr. Blessing expected he would be, but the "pastor" that Elizabeth had prayed he would be. This jarring of expectations was the dynamic within this event that enabled it to disclose a world.[1]

Fourth, this pastoral action remains open to reinterpretation. Pastor Dugan has reinterpreted it many times since it occurred. He has chided himself for not expecting much result from his pastoral action, but he has also taken appropriate credit for persisting in his efforts for Elizabeth to have her day in court. Also, you and I are now in the position of being able to interpret it and perhaps be interpreted by it. As pastors, we might see ourselves in his surprise encounter with Mrs. Parker, and her return in the company of Dr.

Blessing. It is difficult not to feel in ourselves his professional affront, his mounting anger at the doctor and Elizabeth herself. We might also see ourselves at the court hearing, sensing the hostile presence of Dr. Blessing, experiencing the same mixed emotions as to what course of action would be in Elizabeth's best interests, watching her performance with admiration and some wry amusement, and then being utterly taken aback by the judge's announcement of his decision. In these and many other ways, the action is open to reinterpretation and to personal appropriation by persons who were not even there.

THE WISE FOOL

Does our conceptual schema enable us to understand this pastoral action's world-disclosiveness? And does it enable us to place this action in the context of Pastor Dugan's praxis and pastoral self-understanding? Let's look at the latter issue first. As we bring our conceptual schema to bear on this action, it seems clear that Pastor Dugan's action reflects one of the three pastoral images better than the others. He does not work here from a pastoral self-understanding of the wounded healer. He does not encourage Elizabeth to live her pain more deeply and profoundly, and he does not suggest that he felt himself sharing her suffering. Not that he was callous or insensitive; it is just that he knows it would be dishonest of him to claim for himself the pain that Elizabeth was experiencing.

Nor does the action grow out of the shepherd image. In his *conscious* understanding of his role, Pastor Dugan appears to subscribe to the shepherd model. But, in the overall intentionality of his actions in this case, he is much closer to the model of the wise fool. True, he makes use of available resources in the hospital institutional structure, especially the social worker and the legal staff, to provide Elizabeth some assistance. But the shepherd image conveys a pastor who wants to identify the whole range of resources available and bring them to bear on Elizabeth's problems. Pastor Dugan fits this image only very imperfectly. He attempts to mobilize certain available resources in her behalf (e.g., her court hearing). But he does not come across to us as one who wants to serve primarily as Elizabeth's guide, helping her to clarify her various options and identify the whole range of possible resources that might be brought to bear in overcoming the dilemma of her hospitalization. He strikes us as being too uncertain of himself, as not having the clearly formulated plan of operation necessary to be thought of as a shepherding presence in her life. Certainly, she herself does not believe that she would be safe in simply placing her fate in his trust and care. Instead, he comes across as the wise fool. His attitude toward Elizabeth is not that of common sufferer, or the one who offers highly skilled and competent guidance. Rather, he provides simple but reliable loyalty. She may have quit coming to church but he will not abandon her. His interventions in her behalf are based on this fundamental loyalty. The intentionality in his ministry to Elizabeth was less the desire to mobilize resources in her behalf and more the concern to seize the opportunity presented by the possibility of a court hearing to demonstrate a simple loyalty to Elizabeth in her hour of need.

Also, in his approach to Elizabeth's problem, his demeanor was simple and straightforward. He was refreshingly direct with Dr. Blessing. Their professional conflicts of interest clearly bothered him ("Dr. Blessing preempted my conversation with Elizabeth"), but he was able to put them in proper perspective. In fact, in his written account of this action, he acknowledges that he was very deferential in his "confrontation" with Dr. Blessing because "I had already decided that 'boot licking' was my best strategy for dealing with him." This is a comment that the wise fool would make (and the shepherd would not), because it is an admission that he did not mind appearing to be a "fool" in the eyes of Dr. Blessing if this enabled him to assist Elizabeth. Note, too, that Dr. Blessing considered his idea of a court hearing absurd ("the case will be laughed out of court") but this did not daunt him either. He accepted this ridicule because his mind was not on his professional status but on the essential integrity of his plan of action.

In persisting in his view that Elizabeth had a right to her day in court, Pastor Dugan was also quietly prophetic (in the way a "wise fool" is a prophetic figure). He challenged Dr. Blessing's authority to decide whether there would be a hearing or not, and he took the appropriate steps to see that Elizabeth's rights were honored. But he did so not as a thundering prophet *demanding* justice, but more as a supportive prophet trying to do the responsible thing. Thus he acted wisely, but not in a way that drew attention to himself as a "wise" person. His wisdom, in fact, was not the wisdom of prescience, since he actually misjudged how the episode would turn out. It was the wisdom of a prophet's persistence in pursuit of justice, a simple refusal to be swayed from his determination to see that Elizabeth's basic rights were not violated. In this, he was clearly playing the prophet, but in the self-effacing, unassuming manner that the wise fool chooses to play it.

Thus, I would conclude that Pastor Dugan's pastoral self-understanding here was primarily informed by the wise fool model. His actions in relation to Elizabeth, and all the other persons involved in this case, are based on a simple but highly effective concern for truthfulness and honest dealing. While he appears to think of himself in shepherding terms (his conscious perception of himself as pastor), our analysis would suggest that, in his intentionality, he is much closer to the wise fool image.

We cannot determine, on the basis of the case itself, how Pastor Dugan might himself respond to this description of his intentionality. What we can assume is that he is one of a vast number of ministers whose intentionality has moved in a direction that is no longer informed by the pastoral model with which he explicitly identifies. To say this is not to criticize Pastor Dugan and others like him for a lack of congruity between his conscious self-understanding as a pastor and his actual intentionality. On the contrary, it is to recognize that a pastor's intentionality may be "out in front" of his or her conscious pastoral self-understanding.

When we focus on Pastor Dugan's intentionality in this action, and not on his conscious pastoral self-understanding, we find that the revisionist model does the best job of identifying the action's world-disclosure. Pastor Dugan's initial guess as to the meaning of this action has contextual features, inasmuch as he is concerned with the causes of Elizabeth's difficulties and the range of possible resources available to help her overcome them. But as the action begins to unfold, his understanding of the action and its meanings shifts more and more to the revisionist mode. Before long, he is less concerned to put Elizabeth's problem in context, and more interested in trying to find a new perspective from which to view the situation. He exhibits decreasing interest in probing for causes, and when he does attempt an explanation for her problem ("Old woman, if you weren't so selfish, you wouldn't be in this mess"), it is not the careful survey of causes we expect from the contextualist, but the startling insight of the revisionist. The contextualist would find this diagnosis simplistic and rather offbeat: "I would have thought more in terms of her son's death, her blindness, her advanced age, and poor living conditions, not her selfish attitude." Yet this is precisely the point, because the revisionist challenges us to look at problems from an unaccustomed, even unlikely, angle of vision. To suggest that

Elizabeth's problems stem from her selfishness is to probe the under-lying motivations for what she does (Newman), and to judge her actions from God's point of view (Farrar).

Nor does Pastor Dugan approach this action from the perspective of the experientialist, who would want to plunge deeply into Elizabeth's difficulties and to share her burdens. He does not see his presence as communicating to Elizabeth the depths of God's love for her. Nor does he use this occasion to reflect on life's inherent am-biguities. Rather, he is motivated by the desire to get things clear ("Why did you wander out in the street that night?") and wants Elizabeth to have her chance to get things clear ("If Elizabeth has her hearing, this will give her a sense of closure"). He is most reluctant to leave a situation ambiguous if it can be made clear. He much resents being left "in the dark" as to when her court hearing was scheduled, and it disturbs him that the grounds for Elizabeth's hospitalization remain ambiguous.

The assumption behind everything Pastor Dugan does for Elizabeth is that it is better to know the truth of this matter than to be left in the dark, for truth can be an important ally toward restoring her sense of well-being. Thus, his approach to "what happened" in this case is more reflective of the revisionist than either the contex-tual or experiential models.

His understanding of "what may be happening" also reflects the revisionist model. He does not view God's activity in this episode in terms of hope, the contextualist's viewpoint, even though the actions he takes are important for Elizabeth if *she* is not to give up hope. Nor does he view God's activity in terms of grace and love, the experien-tialist's viewpoint, even though the judge's decision could certainly be interpreted as evidence of God's surprising grace and unfailing love. Rather he views God's activity in terms of truth and truthful-ness. He concludes his written account of this action with the ques-tion, What can be said about God on the basis of this episode? And rather than claiming that *he* knows what can be said, he wisely defers to Elizabeth and concludes, "I take consolation when Elizabeth prays, 'You alone, O Lord, can save me,' for I believe she is right." "You alone, O Lord, can save me" is for Pastor Dugan the essential truth revealed through this pastoral action, the essence of its world-disclosive power. It is a simple affirmation of the fact that Elizabeth's deliverance was not the work of any single individual, or even of their collective efforts. Credit for Elizabeth's release belongs to God, and Pastor Dugan wisely recognizes this truth. Moreover, this truth—"you alone, O Lord, can save me"—is a comfort to him as he continues to worry about her safety at home. He does not know why she wandered outside that night and has given up trying to find out. But he does know that she was spared that night and now again in the courtroom. He knows that accidental death at home is always a possibility. But he also senses that in God there is ultimate protection.

It could be objected that this good fit between the revisionist model and the pastoral action is due to the fact that Pastor Dugan was interpreter of his own action. Would the action have the same meaning for other persons influenced by it? I will address this question in chapter 5 when I take up Elizabeth's personal appropriation of this pastoral action. But my preliminary answer is that the action was also, for Elizabeth, much more in the revisionist than the contextual or experiential mode. Her resistance to the hospital staff was ultimately predicated on the conviction that her situation needed to be viewed from a more transcendent point of view. Her "day in court" confirmed for her that God perceived the situation differently from the way the hospital staff saw it. Also, because the judge was the person who actualized God's perspective for her, helping to make it a living reality, he was ultimately in her eyes her "pastor." For Pastor Dugan to be relegated to second-class citizenship in this regard was, in turn, the inevitable fate of the wise fool. But the wise fool is more easily reconciled to this fate than either the shepherd (who not only protects the flock but also jealously guards the leadership prerogatives that go with this protective role), or the wounded healer (who, having shared another's pain, may well resent exclusion from the other's moments of ecstasy and joy). The wise fool wants persons with grievances to receive a fair "hearing." When this happens, the wise fool is fully satisfied, for what distinguishes the *wise* fool from the ordinary fool is that the one desires truth while the other wants attention.

CONCLUSION

In discussing this case involving Elizabeth, I have tried to show how a conceptual schema is vital for understanding a pastoral action. I recognize, of course, that many other conceptual schemas could have been used to understand this particular pastoral action. But this schema enables us to address the two major concerns of our hermeneutical model: the world-disclosive possibilities of the action, and what the action reveals concerning the pastor's praxis and pastoral self-understanding. Thus, it met our expectations of a conceptual schema for pastoral hermeneutics. Also, it was flexible enough that it could be used in the "making-matching, constructing-correcting" style that Hirsch considers essential for hermeneutics. It did not do serious violence to the action, forcing it to yield up meanings that were either not present or merely tangential to "what happened" and "what may be happening" in the case.

What about the problem of false consciousness? Was there an integrity between Pastor Dugan's praxis, as this could be discerned through a single pastoral action, and his pastoral self-understanding? If we had access to a series of pastoral actions by Pastor Dugan, I believe we would discover that he is somewhat in transition in his pastoral self-understanding. Our analysis suggests that he perceives himself to be in the shepherding mode, and that there are some elements of the shepherd image in the pastoral action itself. However, the pastoral image of the wise fool is central to the intentionality of this pastoral action, and this is what our conceptual schema helped us to discover. Does this mean that Pastor Dugan's ministry reflects false consciousness (i.e., lack of integrity between pastoral self-understanding and pastoral intentionality)? As suggested above, I would rather say that his pastoral self-understanding is in a transitional stage, that it is in the process of catching up to his pastoral intentionality. Real false consciousness would be reflected in a minister whose pastoral self-understanding and intentionality are wholly at odds with one another, as when one perceives oneself to be a shepherd but does not provide sound and reliable guidance; a wounded healer, but does not truly share the pain of others; a wise fool, but relates to others in dishonest, deceptive, and highhanded ways. There is a large difference between such incongruity between pastoral self-understanding and pastoral intentionality and incongruity owing to the fact that one's pastoral self-understanding may not have yet caught up with changes in pastoral intentionality.

CHAPTER 5

Form and Metaphor
in
Pastoral Hermeneutics

I have emphasized the world-disclosive possibilities of a pastoral action throughout this study. But I have not yet addressed these two critical questions: (1) What enables a pastoral action to be world-disclosive? That is, what is the *dynamic* that makes such world-disclosure possible? (2) How do we evaluate the world-disclosures of a given pastoral action? That is, how do we assess their *effects* on individuals who appropriate them?

To get at these questions, I propose that we consider how a literary genre addresses the issue of world-disclosure, and then apply what we have learned to pastoral action. The genre I have chosen is the autobiography.

Why autobiography? Other literary genres might serve the same purpose, but there are two good reasons for focusing on autobiography. First, the autobiography is a narrative, or story, and this means that it may have important similarities to pastoral-care-type actions which, as we saw in the case of Elizabeth, typically assume narrative form. (Ricoeur's own interest in narrative, beginning as far back as his *Symbolism of Evil* and culminating most recently in his *Time and Narrative,* is clearly relevant here.)[1] Second, the autobiography, largely because it is narrative, enables us to take up our earlier claim (chapter 2) that *form* and *metaphorical content* are central to the world-disclosiveness of pastoral actions. As I intend to show, certain aspects of the form and metaphorical content of autobiography are remarkably similar to the form and metaphorical content of meaningful pastoral actions. Furthermore, they are central to what makes autobiography world-disclosive. Thus, knowledge of what enables an autobiography to be world-disclosive can be very useful for determining what enables a pastoral action to be world-disclosive. Also, norms developed in autobiography for evaluating world-disclosures can be used for evaluating the world-disclosures of pastoral actions. Let us first take up the issue of form.

THE PARABOLIC EVENT IN AUTOBIOGRAPHY

Autobiographers report a variety of experiences and events in their lives, but most autobiographies also depict a few central events that are unusually arresting. The reader is struck by them and drawn into the story largely because of them. Months or years after reading it, the reader may have forgotten much of the autobiography, but two or three critical events are unforgettable. Readers of Augustine's *Confessions* typically remember the pear-stealing episode, his escape from his mother, and the garden event in which he became a Christian.[2] Readers of Elie Wiesel's *Night* remember the young boy hanging from the gallows and the account of Elie's father's death.[3] These unusually striking episodes are a form within the form of autobiography. I call them "parabolic events" because they have essentially the same structural elements (thematic) and dynamic process (plot) as Jesus' parables.[4] At the risk of oversimplification, I suggest that these are the essential structural elements of his parables.

1. The parable depicts an event in which there is conflict, generally of an interpersonal nature.

2. This conflict results in an altered relationship between the characters in the story. Their relationship at the beginning of the story has become a very different relationship by the end of the story.

3. The meaning of the event is communicated through the story itself. One does not look outside the parable for the "point" of the story. Rather, the story *is* the point.

4. The parable is open-ended. It does not end with a neat and tidy resolution of the conflict situation. The prodigal son is reconciled to his father but the elder son is now estranged. Trusted servants are fired, tenants kill the owner's son, bridesmaids are locked out of a wedding, wedding guests are thrown out, and on and on it goes. As John Dominic Crossan points out, in the parables "reconciliation is no more fundamental a principle than irreconciliation."[5]

5. The parable emphasizes the importance of perceiving what is not readily apparent. Through parables, our customary ways of

perceiving our situation are challenged and upset because they misperceive how God is acting in our world.[6]

The dynamic or plot development of a parable follows from these structural elements. Basically, the parable's dynamic moves toward world-disclosure. It is able to do this because it is clearly metaphorical ("the kingdom of God is like . . ."). Thus, it makes clear from the beginning that the ostensive reference of the story will not exhaust its meaning, that the story will free itself from the limitations of the immediate situation and disclose a larger world (the world of God's activity-in-the-world). This world-disclosure, however, can only be gotten at through the story of human interaction, and it is accessible through the different perspectives ("guesses") listeners bring to the story. The Good Samaritan story, for example, allows different points of entry into the story. We may take the role of the religious leaders who pass by, the despised outcast who stops to help, or the man left bleeding in the ditch.[7] Yet each perspective opens listeners to the story's disclosure of God's activity-in-the-world.

We can see the same structural characteristics and dynamic movement toward world-disclosure in the following typical "parabolic event" in autobiography. This event is taken from Edmund Gosse's *Father and Son*.[8] Young Edmund had just informed his father that he had been invited to a party and his father, opposed to his going for religious and moral reasons, had suggested that they pray about it:

> As I knelt, feeling very small, by the immense bulk of my Father, there gushed through my veins like a wine the determination to rebel. Never before, in all these years of my vocation, had I felt my resistance take precisely this definite form. We rose presently from the sofa, my forehead and the backs of my hands still chafed by the texture of the horsehair, and we faced one another in the dreary light. My father, perfectly confident in the success of what had really been a sort of incantation, asked me in a loud wheedling voice, "Well, and what is the answer which our Lord vouchsafes?" I said nothing, and so my Father, more sharply, continued, "We have asked Him to direct you to a true knowledge of His will. We have desired Him to let you know whether it is, or is not, in accordance with His wishes that you should accept the invitation from the Browns." He positively beamed down at me; he had no doubt of the reply. He was already, I believe, planning some little treat to make up to me for the material deprivation. But my answer came, in the high-piping accents of despair: "The Lord says I may go to the Browns." My father gazed at me in speechless horror. He was caught in his own trap, and though he was certain that the Lord had said nothing of the kind, there was no road open for him but just sheer retreat. Yet surely it was an error in tactics to slam the door.

This episode has all the structural elements of the parable. There is a conflict situation of an interpersonal nature (Edmund vs. his father). Their relationship has been profoundly altered by the end of the story (Edmund has challenged his father, and his father has lost control of the situation). The meaning of the event is communicated through the story (we do not require further commentary on the story from Gosse to enable us to understand it). The story is open-ended (we do not know what will happen to the father-son relationship in the wake of this episode; we only know that it has changed in ways that are fateful for both). Finally, the story is concerned with perceiving what is not readily apparent (his father's assumption that God would not have Edmund go to the Browns' party is not self-evidently true, and Edmund and the readers perceive this).

This episode also has the parable's dynamic movement toward world-disclosure. As we get further into the story, we begin to realize that this is not a mere disagreement between father and son over a party invitation. Rather, what is happening is overshadowed by what may be happening. That the story involves a father and son praying to God contributes to our impression that the story is about something more than meets the eye. But it is not the simple fact that it is *about* God that accounts for its world-disclosive possibilities, for many stories about God have no such possibilities. Rather, its world-disclosiveness has to do with the fact that Edmund has challenged his father's view of how God is *acting* in the world, and this challenge opens a world in which the reader's own assumptions about how God is acting in the world are challenged. If we have assumed that we know the will of God in matters of equally vital importance to us, then this story challenges us by disclosing a world in which our assumptions are no more self-evidently true than those of Edmund's father. It is a world in which no one has a privileged status with regard to discernment of God's will. Thus we begin to envision a new world in which father and son—and we ourselves— kneel before God as *equal* supplicants after "a true knowledge of His will." This is a world in which all supplicants divest themselves of their preconceptions of God's will, and open themselves to what "our Lord" has to say.

PASTORAL ACTIONS AS PARABOLIC EVENTS

In my judgment, meaningful pastoral actions are similar to parabolic events. They share the same structural elements and dynamic process. The pastoral action involving Pastor Dugan and Elizabeth, for example, may be viewed as a parabolic event. In fact, in my earlier discussion, I noted its similarity to Jesus' parable of the judge and the importunate widow.[9]

Take its structural elements. First, it depicts an event in which there is conflict of an interpersonal nature. Elizabeth, Pastor Dugan, Dr. Blessing, and the judge are the principal actors in the conflict, while the social service aide, the hospital social worker, Mrs. Parker, and the lawyer play important but subsidiary roles.

Second, the conflict resulted in an altered relationship between the principal actors. Much like Edmund Gosse's father, Dr. Blessing no longer has control over Elizabeth's future. Pastor Dugan's relationship to Elizabeth remains the same on the surface, but her release is a mixed blessing for him. It means assuming greater responsibility for her welfare. Pastor Dugan's relationship to Dr. Blessing was drastically changed when Elizabeth won her release and the doctor's view that her case would be "laughed out of court" was discredited. But the most decisive change in relationship involved the trio of Elizabeth, Pastor Dugan, and the judge. For, during the court hearing, the judge's role shifted from judge to "pastor," and the judge assumed the role that one suspects Pastor Dugan wishes he could have played: the human catalyst behind God's saving action. Pastor Dugan had to be content with being the one who set the stage for the judge to mediate God's saving power, which is precisely the role of the wise fool. Walter Brueggemann stresses the "wisdom" aspect of this role as he portrays the pastor as a reflective presence, assisting persons in positions of authority and responsibility to enlarge their vision by discerning the "hidden issues" in the decisions they confront.[10] T. S. Eliot, in "The Love Song of J. Alfred Prufrock," captures the element of the fool:

> No! I am not Prince Hamlet, nor was meant to be;
> Am an attendant lord, one that will do
> To swell a progress, start a scene or two,
> Advise the prince; no doubt, an easy tool,
> Deferential, glad to be of use. . . . [11]

No doubt Pastor Dugan saw elements of both in his performance.

Third, the meaning of the event is communicated through the event itself. We do not need to know about Elizabeth's previous life experiences or even what has happened to Elizabeth subsequent to her release in order to understand what this event itself means. In this sense, it is very similar to the episode we quoted from Gosse's autobiography. It was unnecessary for me to provide biographical material on Edmund and his father in order for the reader to understand the episode.

Fourth, the situation remains open-ended. Pastor Dugan worries about Elizabeth's release and what it portends. More important, the conflict between principal actors is also left unresolved. How could Elizabeth and Dr. Blessing ever see eye to eye? If pastoral actions are similar to parabolic events, this means that in many pastoral situations, "reconciliation is no more fundamental a principle than irreconciliation." Stated more boldly, this means that God is not reluctant to take sides.

Fifth, the action shows how our customary ways of perceiving life's situations may be shattered because they misperceive how God is acting-in-the-world. Pastor Dugan was working toward Elizabeth's good adjustment to the hospital while Elizabeth was praying for her release. In the end, events bring Pastor Dugan around to Elizabeth's understanding of how God was at work in this situation. Events confronted him with a God who is able to do more than we ask or think.

The dynamic or plot development of this pastoral action follows from these structural elements. Like parabolic events, its dynamic moves toward world-disclosure. The climax comes in the court hearing when the judge decides in favor of Elizabeth's release, and Elizabeth is able to say, "Thank God, this is what I have prayed for." But also like parabolic events, this world-disclosure can only be gotten at through the story of human interaction. God is not a character in the story but God is, quite literally, what happens in the story, or, more precisely, what "may be happening" in the story.

By comparing pastoral actions to parabolic events in autobiography, we have gained an understanding of what enables a pastoral action to be world-disclosive. Like parables, pastoral actions that are meaningful often shatter our perceptions of how God is at work in our world, and cause us to undergo a restructuring of our perception of what is happening in our world. We now take a radically different view of these two fundamental questions: Where in the world is God? What is becoming of us?

SELF-METAPHORS IN
AUTOBIOGRAPHY

Next, I want to take up the question of *evaluation* of a pastoral action's world-disclosures. How do we assess their *effects* on those who appropriate them? For this, I suggest that we consider the metaphorical content of autobiography and, more specifically, the self-metaphors developed in autobiography.[12]

I take the view that autobiographies are exercises in self-awareness. Thus, if we use autobiography to guide our evaluation of a pastoral action's world-disclosure, our criterion will be whether or not this disclosure contributes to self-awareness. These world-disclosures may have other effects besides greater self-awareness. But from a Christian perspective increase in self-awareness is an especially important effect of world-disclosures because, ever since Augustine, Christians have believed that as we become more self-aware, our awareness of God also deepens. The two questions, Where in the world is God? and What is becoming of us? are inextricably linked. To address the one is necessarily to address the other.

A major function of self-awareness is to reveal to us something about the *nature* of our self, and whether it is in the process of realization (a generative self) or stagnation (a shrinking self). Awareness of the nature and development of our self can be greatly aided by self-metaphors, such as those made available to us through the autobiographical tradition. Here we move to the whole issue of autobiography as an identifiable genre, one which over the centuries has manifested certain dominant self-metaphors.

In surveying autobiographies from Augustine's *Confessions* to the present, William Howarth suggests that there have been three major types of autobiography.[13] He calls them oratory, drama, and poetry. His analysis of each type focuses on the *writer* (character and motives), the *text* (its methods and techniques), and the *reader* (what claims the text exerts on the reader through its themes and meanings). By naming these types oratory, drama, and poetry, Howarth reveals that he is primarily interested in autobiography as a literary form. Because we are interested here in self-metaphors, I will focus on the dominant self-metaphors in each type of autobiography. I call these the *responsible self* (oratory), the *believable self* (drama), and the *accessible self* (poetry). These three types roughly correspond to three phases in the history of autobiography, with Augustine's *Confessions* introducing the responsible self, the Puritan era of the sixteenth and seventeenth centuries introducing the believable self, and the pietism and romanticism of the late eighteenth and nineteenth centuries introducing the accessible self. In discussing each, I will first briefly summarize Howarth's comments, then develop each self-metaphor in more detail. After that I will relate these three self-metaphors to pastoral action, focusing on the effects of pastoral actions on those who appropriate them. Our question is: Does this pastoral action enable the individuals who appropriate it to become more aware of themselves as responsible, believable, and/or accessible selves, and thus to become more aware of what is becoming of them? Also, given that metaphorical likeness (it is) places unlikeness in even starker relief (it is not), is there greater awareness of themselves as irresponsible, unbelievable, and inaccessible? Obviously, the ultimate purpose of such increase in self-awareness is not to indulge any crass narcissistic urges, but to enable those individuals affected by the pastoral action ultimately to discover where in their world is God.

THE RESPONSIBLE SELF

As examples of the oratory type of autobiography, Howarth cites autobiographies of Augustine, John Bunyan, Edward Gibbon, Henry Adams, and Malcolm X. I would add Dorothy Day's *The Long Loneliness*,[14] and would claim that Bunyan's *Grace Abounding to the Chief of Sinners* is a mixture of this and the dramatic type.[15] In this type of autobiography, the writer's character development is represented through an essentially didactic role. These autobiographers' major purpose is to teach readers certain lessons in life. Their credentials for presuming to teach others is not greater learning, but painful experience (i.e., a previous life of sin and error which they have subsequently renounced). These autobiographers' literary methods and techniques are designed to drive their message home. They tell stories to make a moral point, and use various rhetorical devices of a didactic, exhortative, or oratorical nature to persuade their readers that what they say is sound guidance and thus worthy of serious attention. Through these devices, they put a certain distance between themselves as narrator and as subject of the story, and this serves their larger purpose of depicting their earlier life as one they can no longer endorse.

What effect does this didactic approach have on the reader? Howarth suggests that it is twofold. In the first place, these autobiographies emphasize the importance of *vocation*. These autobiographers portray themselves as having responded to a special summons that has guided their life work, and they impress on their readers the importance of responding to a similar summons in their lives. In the second place, these autobiographies convey the idea that the autobiographer's life has an essential unity that springs from a single source: belief in a superior *force* (usually God) that controls one's career from remembered beginning to anticipated end. They encourage readers to seek a similar unity in their lives.

Howarth points out that autobiographies of this type have strict narrative control. To convey the continuity of their lives, the autobiographers write a narrative that reflects a high level of unity and order. Furthermore, autobiographers of this type do not set out to achieve great thematic complexity. They focus on a single theme—their vocation—and are content to trace its history, even though this means excluding other potentially significant life themes. Howarth says we should not be overly critical of the strict narrative control and relatively simple thematic structure of these autobiographies, because we expect no more and no less from orators whose primary purpose is to preach or persuade. Furthermore, he points out that these autobiographers speak pastorally, as shepherds who are attentive to the aspirations of their listening flock. Thus, while the narrative is about the autobiographer, it is much less self-centered than it appears to be, because it is not a testimony to self but to the God who summons us and continues to guide us through life's way. No wonder that many of these autobiographies often seem more like extended sermons than narrative accounts of a life.

The dominant self-metaphor in these autobiographies is the responsible self. This term, which I borrow from H. Richard Niebuhr's *The Responsible Self,*[16] derives from the fact that this type of self is responding to a summons from God—hence, the *responsible* self. Responsible selves look back on their lives prior to the response to God as absolute irresponsibility. In effect, sin is understood as irresponsibility, while fidelity to one's vocation is evidence that one is no longer controlled by sin. The responsible self is a somewhat divided person, even as in autobiography of this type the narrator and protagonist are clearly distinguishable. On a day-to-day basis, this division is between those aspects of life that are considered relevant to one's vocation and those considered irrelevant or tangential to it. As for the overall course of one's life, this division is between one's current life of responsibility and previous life of irresponsibility. The previous life has to be disowned, which can mean disowning one's past self and even the other selves who shaped one's past. Thus, responsible selves are very conscious of problems of estrangement and interpersonal and intergenerational conflict, and often see their vocation as overcoming division and effecting reconciliation.

Responsible selves recognize that their response to God entails responsibility for other persons. Others look to them for guidance and moral instruction, and they in turn ignore their own cares in order to provide it. When others are tempted to be irresponsible, the responsible self weans them away from this temptation, and often answers for them to those who have authority over them. Responsible selves recognize that they are sometimes irresponsible themselves. But the rationale for calling them the responsible self is not their faithfulness as such, but their change in *status* from individuals who previously only answered for themselves but now answer to God. They are very conscious that the change effected in their lives (whether viewed as a conversion or some other type of personal transformation) is a change in status, and thus as objectively real and permanent as anything in life can be.

In my view, the pastoral image of the *shepherd* is a working out of the pastoral implications of the responsible self. Like responsible selves, shepherds attend to the needs of those for whom they assume responsibility. But also like responsible selves, shepherds recognize that they cannot force the others to accept their guidance, so they seek to make it attractive as well as authoritative. Its attractiveness is its promise of greater well-being for those who listen, and its authoritativeness is the fact that the shepherd knows intimately the perils to which the flock are subject. When we link the pastoral image of shepherd to the responsible self, we recognize that a dominant theme of the shepherd model is responsibility. The shepherd assumes responsibility for the sheep (they "hear his voice"), but not to the extent that they are no longer responsible for themselves. Hiltner's dictum "The pastor helps others to help themselves" captures the shepherd's ultimate objective.

THE BELIEVABLE SELF

As examples of autobiography as drama, Howarth cites Benvenuto Cellini, James Boswell, Benjamin Franklin, William Carlos Williams, and Sean O'Casey. In these autobiographies the author's character is represented through an essentially theatrical role. These autobiographers do not present themselves as a lesson to others, but as performing artists whose idiosyncrasies evoke the audience's attention. While the oratorical autobiographers take themselves very seriously, dramatic autobiographers engage in considerable self-mockery. They play many different roles in the course of their narratives, they hide behind masks, and portray themselves with a mixture of fakery and truth which they fully anticipate their readers will "see through." Their motive is not to teach but to win approval for themselves, and to achieve this they walk a tightrope between addressing their own interests, and responding to the readers' demand for an entertaining story. In contrast to the orators, these autobiographers relate life incidents not for the purpose of pointing out a moral but simply to create a believable character. This means giving considerable attention to small and seemingly insignificant details about themselves. Often, these details are more valuable than direct self-testimony in enabling the reader to sense the truth about the author. The character is created with considerable deception, impersonation, and disguise, but the reader senses that such playing fast and loose with facts is basically honest in its deceit and thus reveals a more fundamental truth about the character. Essentially the same kind of exaggeration and posing is necessary in stage drama to convey the essence of the character being portrayed.

The literary style of these autobiographies is not to prove anything, but to portray a colloquial, conversational, and apparently spontaneous mind. To sustain interest in their characters, they create dialogue, stress spectacle, and use various theatrical devices (choric response, asides, clever plotting, and so forth). Their intention is not to make a convincing point, but to create and sustain action. And because their purpose is not didactic, the roles of autobiographer as narrator and as autobiographical subject are well integrated. These autobiographers are the directors in a play in which they are the central character. Thus, the narrative unfolds like a well-made play, with the author's various personae adding up to an overall consistency of character. However, if the life has artistic consistency, it clearly lacks the vocational consistency of the autobiographer as orator. Because these autobiographers are able to play many roles, their multiple talents lead them in many different directions, from art to public life. Moreover, unlike the orator, they do not bow to superior forces, but portray themselves as individuals who simply want to play their part well at any given time and place on the stage of human life.

As to what the narrative communicates to the reader, Howarth says that dramatists do not have a theme as such because they are actors, not teachers. However, they do communicate a strong commitment to life and a passion for engagement in the world's affairs. They have nothing to say about death. Nor do they seek to communicate any deep conviction about life's meaning and purpose. If there is a superior force guiding human affairs, this has little if anything to do with the story they want to tell. But this does not mean life has no meaning for them. They offer various clues throughout the narrative which they believe may unlock for the reader some of the riddles and enigmas of life. They offer penetrating insights and wise counsel in lieu of a sustained, consistent message.

The dominant self-metaphor in these autobiographies is what I call the *believable self*. The believable self has a strong commitment to truth. As Howarth shows, the dramatic autobiographers create a believable character by attending above all to matters of truth. They are not reluctant to pose, exaggerate, stretch facts, and so forth as long as they know that the reader will see through all this and perceive the truth that it communicates. Believable selves will feign stupidity, for example, if they feel confident that this will not be perceived by the reader as *real* stupidity but actually as wisdom in disguise. Furthermore, believable selves do not have any use for abstract truth. Their forte is truth-in-action. They want others to perceive that they do not merely talk about truth but actually embody it. Also, the point is not that they should always be acting, but that they should be truthful, and this means there are times when they simply refuse to act.

Believable selves are also very attentive to issues of role consistency. It is through the roles they assume (even more than the vocation they adopt) that they communicate their believability to others. Thus they are careful to select from their many roles those that best communicate the essence of their character. Believability is a matter of consistency as well as truth, and such consistency is best reflected in whether the roles they have played in life have a meaningful relation to one another. If their movement from one role to another seems random or arbitrary, or if the roles they play are obviously discrepant, their believability is undermined. Their lives must communicate the fact that, while they have played many different roles, many simultaneously, the overall thrust of their lives is a consistency of character.

I see the pastoral image of the *wise fool* as the working out of the pastoral implications of the believable self. Through personal simplicity, loyalty, and quiet prophecy, the wise fool comes across as a believable, credible person. Also, like the believable self, this pastoral image emphasizes the importance of truth-in-action. The wise fool suspects abstract ideas and concepts, and instead seeks to embody truth through role performance and role consistency. Wise fools give the impression of a lack of sophistication or of limited knowledge, but this is usually a disguise that they employ in order to achieve objectives that might otherwise fail. The shepherd's ministry is motivated by a sense of responsibility, and therefore reflects much concern about determining the scope and boundaries of their responsibility (the question of pastoral referral is of central importance to shepherds). The wise fool's ministry is dominated by a strong commitment to life, and therefore reflects much concern about what makes for abundant living. In contrast to shepherds, wise fools are attuned more to issues of performance than status and are, in fact, inclined toward a certain lack of deference for status claims and needs, including their own. Wise fools may be somewhat more self-indulgent than shepherds because their concern is not Did I do the responsible thing? but Did I perform my role effectively? On the other hand, they are less likely to impose their will on those to whom they minister. Shepherds have visions which they hope others will come to share, while wise fools have insights which they hope others will not dismiss.

THE ACCESSIBLE SELF

As examples of the autobiography-as-poetry type, Howarth cites Jean-Jacques Rousseau, Henry Thoreau, Walt Whitman, William Butler Yeats, and James Agee. I would also add C. S. Lewis's *Surprised by Joy*,[17] though it has elements of the dramatic type as well. In this type, the autobiographers do not present themselves as teachers or as characters on a stage, but as individuals engaged in continuing self-study. They confess that they do not understand themselves, and have trouble making sense of the experiences in their lives that they relate in the autobiography. But, in the course of their narrative, they try various kinds of experiments designed to gain access to the self. Some of these experiments work, others fail. But the experimentation has its own intrinsic interest and value. Unlike the oratory type, these autobiographers suppress moral judgments and are diffident about stating their beliefs or convictions. Unlike the dramatic type, they are quite inward. The dramatic type may "hide behind a mask" but expects that the mask itself will be revealing. For them, life is a stage. In contrast, the poetic types withdraw into themselves and create an inner landscape where they interact, through imagination and reverie, with significant figures in their lives, including individuals personally known to them, and individuals encountered through reading and conversation with others.

If oratory types want to communicate the unity of their lives, and thus exercise strict narrative control, poetic types make frequent changes of course in the narrative. They often confess that what originally motivated them to write is no longer compelling, acknowledge that they do not fully understand their purpose in writing the book, and present themselves as a serial image for which their readers have to provide the missing continuity or thematic unity. In effect, the narrative reflects an ongoing search for a "true self" and little sense of having found it. Rather, it displays continuing experiments in the search. These are illuminating, but they are also very tentative.

As to literary style, the poetic autobiographers do not so much report previous experiences as reappropriate them. They seek words and phrases that recapture experiences and give them an entirely new significance. Meanings emerge from these experiences, slowly and organically, as ideas and images find each other. The object is not to present the overall structure or pattern of the life. Instead, it is to communicate the sense that the autobiography is an ongoing process of self-discovery, one that will not end when the narrative itself is brought to a close. The poetic autobiographer is less concerned to persuade than the orator and to entertain than the dramatist, and relies instead on the compelling power of images and metaphors.

The themes communicated to the reader are essentially paradoxical ones. Where the orator finds grounds for conviction, and the dramatist sorts through life's puzzles and enigmas to find valuable truths, the poet sees fundamental paradox, disparity, and ambiguity. This places "authorial obligations" on the reader to discover whatever wholeness or connectedness the autobiographical self may possess. The reader is given this responsibility not because the autobiographers skillfully maneuver themselves out of it, but because these are simply matters that exceed their understanding. While it is tempting to view poetic autobiographers as possessing greater self-awareness than the other types, this is not necessarily the case. Certainly, they have greater difficulty in communicating it. The other types have at their disposal various rhetorical and theatrical techniques to assist them in communicating their self-awareness to others, whereas the poetic autobiographers create these methods in an experimental fashion as they go along. On the other hand, this serves the poetic autobiographers' tendency to celebrate the process of becoming. These autobiographies do communicate a sense of vocation, not however as a calling but as a creative act that autobiography itself demands. More than for the other two types, the actual writing of the autobiography is a means of personal fulfillment.

The dominant self-metaphor in these autobiographies is what I call the *accessible self*, a term suggested by Erving Goffman's work on the presentation of the self.[18] The poetic autobiographers are concerned with how to gain access to their essential selves, and recognize that this is a complex problem that cannot be solved by casual reflection. Thus, the accessible self is characterized by continuing self-study. The self becomes an object of careful scrutiny as though placed under a microscope. Accessible selves are likely to say that they are discovering new facets of themselves, or finding things out about themselves that they hardly knew existed. Past experiences are scrutinized for what secrets they may yield about the self, and the self is thought of as emerging from shadows into light, or as a more clearly identifiable figure against a rather hazy background.

Accessible selves are aware of being at fault, but their sense of wrongness is quite different from that of responsible and believable selves. For the responsible self, sin is irresponsibility; for the believable self it is deception. For the accessible self, it is the sense of being imprisoned, unable to "open" oneself to opportunities for becoming a more full-bodied self. Accessible selves see themselves as developing, growing, evolving selves, but do not like to use imagery of status or roles to describe this process. Rather, they use imagery of awareness ("I am more aware of myself than before") and emergence ("My real self is finally coming out"). Change is registered by serial images that reveal new facets of the self while preserving or modulating those previously known.

Accessible selves have a profound sense of being incomplete, seeking fulfillment but never, except in rare ecstatic moments, experiencing it. If others perceive them as coherent and unified selves, they may accept this as an accurate external observation, but what impresses them more is how incomplete and perhaps even fragmented they are, a kaleidoscope of images constantly shifting in their relationship to one another. Aware of this incompleteness, accessible selves do not feel personally qualified to guide others, but are content if they can simply make themselves "available" to others. In the same way that the reader must assume some authorial obligations for the text, other persons must determine how *they* want to relate to the accessible self. Furthermore, because accessible selves are aware of being incomplete, they are much more likely than the other types to seek fulfillment through other selves. Responsible and believable selves have a clearer sense of the distinction between self and other selves, whereas accessible selves are so aware of the interdependence of selves that this distinction between self and others sometimes seems artificial and forced.

In my view, the pastoral image of the *wounded healer* develops the pastoral implications of the accessible self. Wounded healers make themselves accessible to others, and try to do so on the other person's terms. To become accessible to others, they recognize the need to become accessible to themselves, and know that this is a difficult task. As Henri Nouwen puts it, "In order to be available to others, a man has to be available to himself first of all. And we know how extremely difficult it is to be available to ourselves, to have our own experiences at our disposal. We know how selective our self-understanding really is."[19] Still, wounded healers commit themselves to becoming more accessible to themselves and thereby to other selves, fully aware that this means becoming intimately acquainted with pain and suffering. To become accessible to others means not only sharing their joys and satisfactions but also their sorrow, their brokenness and incompleteness, and their emptiness. Wounded healers may not be able to promise release from suffering, but their very availability has its own healing power. Wounded healers do not make important claims for what they are doing, and in fact often seem more engaged in pastoral experimentation than formulating methods and techniques. Yet this very diffidence can be attractive to those who are turned off by the pastoral image of the shepherd, with its emphasis on assuming responsibility for others. The wounded healer replaces the language of responsibility with the language of availability and presence. Also, while the shepherd image has an affinity for *ethics* (especially the ethics of responsibility), and the wise fool for *morality* (especially the personal virtues of simplicity and loyalty), the wounded healer has an affinity for spirituality (especially prayer and other acts of devotion and obedience whose intent is to make oneself accessible to God).

SELF-METAPHORS AND
PASTORAL ACTIONS

Two general comments about these self-metaphors are in order before we relate them to pastoral actions. First, these three "selves" are not merely descriptive of ourselves as we really are, but metaphors that disclose the self we envision ourselves to be. Some of us may already reflect one or another of these metaphors to a

FIGURE B
A CONCEPTUAL SCHEMA FOR EVALUATING PASTORAL ACTIONS

	EVALUATING PERSONAL APPROPRIATION		EVALUATING PASTORAL INTENTIONALITY
Self-Metaphors	*Evidence of Growth in Self-Awareness*	*Pastoral Models*	*Intentionality*
The Responsible Self	1) greater fidelity to life's vocation 2) more responsive to God 3) seeks reconciliation with others	Shepherd	1) acts responsibly toward others 2) allows others freedom to act
The Believable Self	1) greater role consistency 2) more attentive to meaning of life events 3) acts more truthfully in relations with others	Wise Fool	1) contributes to enrichment of lives of others 2) acts with consistency
The Accessible Self	1) new self-discoveries 2) more aware of interdependence of self and other selves 3) more accessible to others	Wounded Healer	1) emotionally available to others 2) open to self-examination

considerable extent. After all, metaphors depend on there being some likeness between them and the known reality. But these metaphors also disclose a way of being-in-the-world that we experience as partially unknown, perhaps even alien to us. Furthermore, each metaphor reveals what in us impedes fuller entry into the world they disclose. For the responsible self, it is a continuing attraction to the life of irresponsibility. For the believable self, it is a continuing attraction to deception and lies. For the accessible self, it is a continuing imprisonment of the self within itself (what Erikson calls "self-absorption"). Thus, orienting ourselves to the world they disclose means disorientation with respect to the world we already inhabit. (See Figure B.)

Second, since autobiography as a genre is deeply rooted in the Christian tradition, these three self-metaphors are legitimate ways for Christians to orient their lives. None is inherently superior from a Christian point of view than the others. If we take the evolution of the autobiography genre as our guide, it is certainly true that the first autobiography, Augustine's *Confessions*, puts forward the ideal of the responsible self, thus seeming to make this metaphor normative for Christians. But the genius of the *Confessions*, what makes it a Christian classic of the highest order, is that it also gives expression to the other two metaphors which were developed more fully later. Augustine wants to be perceived as believable by his readers (hence the heavy documentation of his previous life of irresponsibility), and experiments with the autobiographical form as a means of making himself accessible to God, so that God may become more accessible to him ("If I had hidden myself from God, I would have hidden God from myself"). Thus, all three self-metaphors are legitimate from a Christian point of view, and are valid for evaluating the effects of specific pastoral actions. Figure B provides criteria for evaluating pastoral actions in terms of their appropriation and intentionality.

But how are these self-metaphors employed in evaluating pastoral actions? I suggest that we use three categories for guiding our evaluation: *illumination, transformation,* and *conversion.* The illumination category concerns persons who, by virtue of a disclosive pastoral action, become more like their dominant self-metaphor, whether responsible, believable, or accessible. The pastoral action is therefore evaluated for its contribution to individuals' greater approximation to the self-metaphor that already orients them to the world. Are they able, through personal appropriation of this action, to recognize themselves more clearly in this metaphor? We would not expect a perfect correspondence between this appropriation and the self-metaphor. Indeed, pastoral actions may be more influential for us when they disclose *dissimilarity* between ourselves and the metaphor. But we can look for evidence of illumination, a closer likeness between the self that we are and the self that the metaphor mirrors.

The second category is transformation, which occurs when a disclosive pastoral action (or series of such actions) effects a change from one dominant self-metaphor to another. Often, this is a perception-shattering experience, as one's accustomed orientation to the world gives way, either temporarily or more permanently, to a new orientation (as when a predominantly "responsible self" becomes an "accessible self").[20]

The third category is conversion, which occurs when a disclosive pastoral action (or series of such actions) causes an individual who previously was not oriented to any of these self-metaphors to become oriented to one of them. In this case, a person who was previously an irresponsible, unbelievable, or inaccessible self becomes a responsible, believable, or accessible self.

Autobiography itself abounds with all three categories; each may function in the narrative as a parabolic event. A responsible self, like Dorothy Day awaiting the birth of her child, discovers new dimensions of what responsibility for others means (illumination). Or an accessible self, like C.S. Lewis prior to his adoption of the Christian faith, becomes a believable self (transformation). Or an irresponsible self, like Augustine before his conversion to Christianity, becomes a responsible self (conversion). Not all such changes are directly precipitated by pastoral actions, for the disclosive power of God is certainly not captive to ecclesiastical structures. But when pastoral actions are disclosive, we may look for evidence of one or more of these effects, whether illumination, transformation, or conversion.

SELF-METAPHORS AND CHRISTIAN REALIZATION

As we look at the case of Pastor Dugan and Elizabeth, I would suggest that here we have evidence of the illuminating mode, which is less dramatic than the others but a no less significant effect of a disclosive pastoral action. Let us focus here on Elizabeth, the one for whom the event was most immediately disclosive.

In my view, the dynamics of this pastoral action reflect a clash between two self-metaphors: the responsible and the believable self. The responsible self is prominent in the ostensive situation while the believable self is central to its world-disclosive possibilities. The major theme of the action prior to the court hearing is responsibility. What is our responsibility to Elizabeth? Is she capable of assuming responsibility for herself? Has she acted irresponsibly in the past? Who would assume responsibility for her if she were released? But when the court hearing began, the dynamic process changed from responsibility to believability. The issue came down to whose perspective is the most credible, Dr. Blessing's or Elizabeth's, and the judge decided in favor of Elizabeth. Questions of responsibility were forced into the background or treated as relatively incidental, and believability became the overriding issue. If Elizabeth is not considered by the hospital to be mentally ill, what is the rationale for not releasing her? In making this shift from responsibility to believability, the action itself became potentially world-disclosive. It was no longer hostage to the immediate situation.

The individual who was able to capitalize on this shift was Elizabeth. Unlike Dr. Blessing or even Pastor Dugan, she was not concerned with the problem of responsibility. She may have sensed that because of her age and her blindness there was not much point in claiming that she could be responsible for herself. But if she could not be the responsible self, she could be the believable self, and this is clearly how she comported herself throughout the episode. Her expressions of intense desire to return home were convincing to Pastor Dugan and this, together with credible evidence that there was nothing wrong with her mind, convinced him that these desires should not be ignored. Furthermore, when she appeared before the judge, she was believable in her very artfulness. To Pastor Dugan, she was playing a role, one designed to secure the judge's sympathy for her plight. In calling the judge "pastor" and then proceeding to tell him what she "had been praying for," she may well have been indulging in a bit of chicanery. But this does not mean that she was being untruthful. On the contrary, she was able to pose in this fashion because she knew that the judge would see through all this and perceive the truth that it communicated: that she was a woman of unbroken spirit and resourcefulness who should be allowed to live according to her desires. The believable self has a strong commitment to life, and the role that Elizabeth played in the court hearing was consistent with that commitment.

Elizabeth was oriented to the believable self in this episode, but is there evidence that this reflected increase in self-awareness? Or was she simply repeating the same role she had played many times before? No doubt, she had been more oriented toward the believable self than the responsible self for much of her life, at least since becoming blind, which significantly reduced her capacity to be "responsible" for herself in more customary ways. Also, her manner of relating to others suggests she was not strongly oriented toward the accessible self. But she appears to have experienced new dimensions of the believable self through this threatening experience. Her hospitalization and the court hearing gave her an opportunity to demonstrate truth-in-action, not just to talk about how only God could save her but to give this truth intentional force. In this way, Elizabeth experienced illumination, increased likeness to the self-metaphor to which her life was already oriented. The pastoral action effected neither a transformation nor a conversion, yet it was profoundly disclosive. As Elizabeth appropriated the action, allowed herself to be interpreted by it, she became aware of dimensions of her dominant self-metaphor that she had not experienced before. And most importantly, she also discovered new grounds for "believing" in God.

THE BIBLICAL FOUNDATION OF
SELF-METAPHORS

These three self-metaphors are reflected in the autobiographical form, which is an integral part of the Christian tradition. But some readers may feel that this is not a strong enough argument for using these self-metaphors as norms to assess individuals' appropriation of pastoral action. Believing that the autobiographical tradition is not a central stream in the Christian tradition, or that it has of late been subject to various secularizing influences, they would be more willing to accord these self-metaphors an evaluative status if they were based on an undeniably central element in the Christian tradition, such as the Bible.

Fortunately the three self-metaphors are also supported by biblical understandings of the self-in-relation-to-God. The dynamic interaction between God and self is often expressed in the Bible in terms of mutual expectations of responsibility, believability, and accessibility. In fact, it is quite possible that these self-metaphors derive ultimately from biblical understandings of God as responsible God, believable God, and accessible God. These three "models" of God-in-the-world are in turn made up of various more transient biblical "metaphors" of God. Like our three self-metaphors, these "models" of God survive their more occasional metaphors, having uncommon "staying power." In many biblical texts, God is praised for being responsible, believable, and accessible, and is criticized when circumstances suggest that God has acted irresponsibly, or has become unbelievable or inaccessible. A variety of biblical texts illustrate this.

For example, the three major wisdom texts (Proverbs, Ecclesiastes, and Job) explore, respectively, the responsibility, believability, and accessibility of God. Proverbs suggests that God acts responsibly, even though individuals may cite circumstantial evidence to the contrary (Why do the wicked prosper?), through the creation and maintenance of a consistent moral order. Ecclesiastes struggles with the question of whether the way God acts toward us is believable. The preacher does not doubt God's existence, but wonders about God's credibility as he reflects on the way the world functions. In the end, he affirms God's believability, but acknowledges that what undergirds this affirmation is his profound sense of God's inscrutability, which human wisdom cannot penetrate. Job is primarily concerned with God's accessibility. Job wants to meet with God, to see God face to face in order to establish his personal integrity. Thus, the three major wisdom books in the Bible focus on the same three self-metaphors, exploring attributions of responsibility, believability, and accessibility to God, the Ultimate Self.

The Synoptic Gospels follow the same basic pattern in their representations of Jesus as God's self-disclosure. Matthew emphasizes that Jesus responded to his divine mission, and challenged his disciples to do the same. Luke focuses on the grounds for believing that Jesus is Christ and thus for Luke the credibility and reliability of his account of the life of Jesus is critical. Mark describes how the real identity of Jesus as Christ was often hidden, and is therefore profoundly concerned with the theme of God's accessibility. Thus, the three Synoptic Gospels also focus on the same three self-metaphors, presenting Jesus as the responsible Christ, the believable Christ, and as the Christ whose very hiddenness paradoxically enables him to be the accessible Christ.

Then there is the story of Ruth. The three major figures in this story correspond to the three self-metaphors we have been discussing. Naomi reflects the responsible self as she assumed responsibility for finding her daughter-in-law a home in her adopted land. Ruth reflects the believable self through her loyalty to Naomi and consistency in her actions toward Boaz. Boaz reflects the accessible self in opening his heart to Ruth and thereby perpetuating the name of her dead husband.

There are similar instances of the interaction of the three self-metaphors in Jesus' life and teachings. In the story of Mary sitting at the feet of Jesus while her sister is occupied with domestic chores, Martha is portrayed as a responsible self, while Mary is the believable self through her simple commitment to truth and loyalty to Jesus, and Jesus is the accessible self, making himself available to her and, by implication, to anyone who wants to come and have conversation with him. A similar mutuality between the accessible and believable self, at the apparent expense of the responsible self, is evident in Jesus' parable of the prodigal son, where the eldest son is the responsible self, the youngest son eventually becomes the believable self, and the father reveals himself as the accessible self.

In line with John Dominic Crossan's suggestion that parable is the binary opposite of myth,[21] we might say that all three parables (the story of Ruth, Naomi, and Boaz; the story of Mary, Martha, and Jesus; and the story of the father and his two sons) stand in direct opposition to the Garden of Eden myth, in which the three participants (Adam, Eve, and Tempter) acted as irresponsible, deceptive, and imprisoned selves. The Tempter is certainly the deceiver, the polar opposite of the believable self, while Adam and Eve are irresponsible at the beginning of the story (eating from the forbidden tree), and this leads them to become inaccessible selves, prisoners in their world, at the end of the story (as they attempt to hide, making themselves inaccessible to God).

Admittedly, my proposal that the major wisdom texts, the Synoptic Gospels, and various biblical stories reflect our self-metaphors is what Ricoeur calls a "guess." It would have to be supported by much more careful analysis of these texts than is possible here. But this proposal helps to make the fundamental point that the three self-metaphors are consistent with biblical understandings of God (the Ultimate Self) and Christ (the Self-for-Others). This means that our evaluation of appropriations of pastoral actions in terms of the three self-metaphors is consistent with biblical understandings of God-in-relation-to-other-selves. No doubt, many other self-metaphors would also have their genesis in God. But these three at least begin to capture the complexity, if not the fullness of God, having remarkable similarities to the Trinitarian formula itself. (Yet startling disclosures may occur when we challenge the usual identification of the

Father with the responsible self, Christ with the believable self, and the Holy Spirit with the accessible self.) And, of course, the same complex relationship holds for the three "persons" in the hermeneutical process. If authors are primarily responsible selves, texts mainly believable selves, and readers primarily accessible selves, each also shares the dominant characteristic of the other. On the basis of analogies commonly drawn between God, texts, and human persons, we should therefore expect that persons, created in the image of God and shaped by the Word of God, would also reflect all three self-metaphors—though in varying degrees of likeness and form.

CONCLUSION

In chapter 2, where I identified the elements necessary for a hermeneutical model of pastoral care, I indicated that it seemed unfeasible to develop a flow chart whose intent would be to describe the hermeneutical process from beginning to end. On the other hand, we have now come to the point where we might, at least, attempt to schematize the model (see Figure C), indicating its various interrelationships. The value of such a schematization is twofold: (1) It will provide a graphic illustration of how the various elements of our model fit together; and (2) it will help us to identify the limits of a hermeneutical model of pastoral care (i.e., what it necessarily excludes from its purview).

In developing this schema, I have not attempted to maintain a firm distinction between those elements of the model that are inherent in any hermeneutical model of pastoral care, and those that are simply part of the conceptual schematization inherent in this particular model. However, I would suggest that *major headings* under the three dimensions of *structure* (pastoral self-understanding, genre, self-awareness), *process* (pastoral orientation, interpretive process, disclosive event), and *focus* (intentionality, interpretation, evaluation) are inherent in any hermeneutical model of pastoral care, while the elements indicated in the six triangles are aspects of the conceptual schema developed for this particular study, and thus could be replaced with other categories. It should also be noted that, under "meaningful pastoral action," I mean by "genre" not a literary genre (such as autobiography) but a pastoral care genre (such as hospital visitation, premarital counseling, crisis counseling, and the like). Since in this study I focused on only one such genre (hospital visitation), and then used it only illustratively, much more work

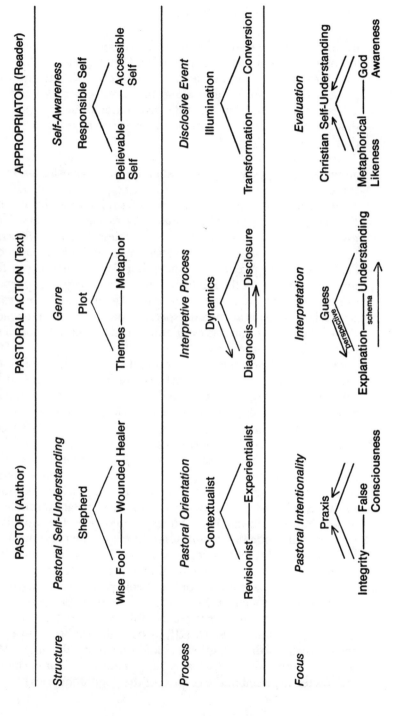

FIGURE C
ELEMENTS FOR A PASTORAL HERMENEUTIC

	PASTOR (Author)	PASTORAL ACTION (Text)	APPROPRIATOR (Reader)
Structure	*Pastoral Self-Understanding*	*Genre*	*Self-Awareness*
	Shepherd	Plot	Responsible Self
	Wise Fool —— Wounded Healer	Themes —— Metaphor	Believable Self —— Accessible Self
Process	*Pastoral Orientation*	*Interpretive Process*	*Disclosive Event*
	Contextualist	Dynamics	Illumination
	Revisionist —— Experientialist	Diagnosis —— Disclosure	Transformation —— Conversion
Focus	*Pastoral Intentionality*	*Interpretation*	*Evaluation*
	Praxis	Guess	Christian Self-Understanding
	Integrity —— False Consciousness	Explanation —perspective—schema— Understanding	Metaphorical Likeness —— God Awareness

needs to be done on this aspect of the model. I have given more attention in this study to the "pastor" and "appropriator" than to the structure and process of the "text." However, the diagram does provide the categories (genre and interpretive process) and their subcategories (the triangles indicated under these categories), so that the basic blueprint is provided for further explorations along these lines.

Recent efforts to relate the Bible to pastoral care and counseling already provide a valuable foundation for such explorations. In fact, three recent books in this vein focus, respectively, on the three elements of genre and interpretive process indicated in the chart. Eugene Peterson's *Five Smooth Stones for Pastoral Work* is oriented toward the plot structure, William B. Oglesby's *Biblical Themes for Pastoral Care* focuses on the thematics, while my *Biblical Approaches to Pastoral Counseling* centers on metaphor. While these books focus mainly on the uses of the Bible for dynamic and diagnostic purposes, our examples of self-metaphors in biblical texts, as well as my earlier discussions of biblical forms, especially parables, suggest that the Bible is extremely valuable for identifying the disclosive possibilities of pastoral actions.[22]

Finally, the diagram informs us that there is much about pastoral care that a hermeneutical model necessarily leaves out. Our hermeneutical model, for example, does not take into account the *personalities* of either pastor or appropriator. By limiting ourselves to "self-understanding" and "self-awareness," we do not say anything about the personal characteristics of the individuals involved in the pastoral action. Thus, questions as to what personality structures are most conducive to initiating or appropriating pastoral actions are not addressed. Similarly, our hermeneutical model has nothing to say about what *social contexts* are conducive to meaningful pastoral action. However, a valuable next step would be to develop linkages between our models of pastoral self-understanding and metaphors of self-awareness, and metaphors of the Christian community.[23]

And, finally, our hermeneutical model does not address in any systematic way the many important theological and ethical concerns that it begins to touch on. By conceiving the appropriation of pastoral actions in terms of the three metaphors of the responsible self, believable self, and accessible self, we have already begun to address the concerns of theological ethics and devotional theology. Moreover, our emphasis on "disclosure" may require that our hermeneutical model be placed in the context of theological theories of revelation, and our emphasis on the self-formative effects of pastoral actions may prompt us to invoke theological concepts of sanctification and holiness. But, as indicated in the introduction to this volume, my primary goal here has been the very practical objective of refurbishing the "action-reflection" model employed in clinical pastoral education and many other educational contexts in pastoral care. My interest has not been to use hermeneutics to build bridges to the theological disciplines. Nor have I atempted to wed pastoral hermeneutics to specific psychological theories or schools of thought, as Charles Gerkin does in *The Living Human Document*. What I have tried to demonstrate is that interpretation of pastoral actions, while not a simple task, is a necessary one. For pastoral actions are appropriated through interpretation and therefore those that are not interpreted are like a seed that "fell on the rock; and as it grew up, it withered away, because it had no moisture" (Luke 8:6).

Notes

INTRODUCTION

1. See, for example, John Patton, "Clinical Hermeneutics: Soft Focus in Pastoral Counseling and Theology," *Journal of Pastoral Care* 35 (1981): 157–68, and Charles V. Gerkin, *The Living Human Document: Re-Visioning Pastoral Counseling in a Hermeneutical Mode* (Nashville: Abingdon Press, 1983). Professor Gerkin's book came to my attention after this manuscript was completed. I would like to have taken his work into account in this book. However, I believe these two efforts are complementary since he is especially interested in providing a hermeneutical understanding of pastoral counseling while I am more concerned here with a more general approach to pastoral care. In his epilogue, Gerkin cites the need for a hermeneutical theory of "pastoral care in the parish." So, in a sense, this book may be seen as the "next step" in the enterprise that his book has so ably initiated.

2. See Alastair V. Campbell, *Rediscovering Pastoral Care* (Philadelphia: Westminster Press, 1981) and Donald Capps, *Life Cycle Theory and Pastoral Care* (Philadelphia: Fortress Press, 1983), chap. 5.

CHAPTER 1

1. Norman Perrin, *Jesus and the Language of the Kingdom* (Philadelphia: Fortress Press, 1976), 2.

2. My primary sources for the following discussion are Paul Ricoeur, *Interpretation Theory: Discourse and the Surplus of Meaning* (Fort Worth: Texas Christian University Press, 1976); Charles E. Reagan and David Stewart, eds., *The Philosophy of Paul Ricoeur: An Anthology of His Work* (Boston: Beacon Press, 1978); Paul Ricoeur, *The Conflict of Interpretations: Essays in Hermeneutics,* ed. Don Ihde (Evanston, Ill.: Northwestern University Press, 1974); Paul Ricoeur, *Essays on Biblical Interpretation,* ed. Lewis S. Mudge (Philadelphia: Fortress Press, 1980).

3. Paul Ricoeur, "The Model of the Text: Meaningful Action Considered as a Text," *Social Research* 38 (Autumn 1971): 536.

4. Ibid.

5. Ibid.

6. Ibid.

7. Ricoeur, *Essays on Biblical Interpretation*, 73–118.
8. Ibid., 87.
9. Donald Capps, *Biblical Approaches to Pastoral Counseling* (Philadelphia: Westminster Press, 1981).
10. Ibid., 108–10.
11. Sallie McFague, *Metaphorical Theology* (Philadelphia: Fortress Press, 1982), 13.
12. Ibid., 46–47.
13. Paul Ricoeur, "Listening to the Parables of Jesus," in *The Philosophy of Paul Ricoeur*, 242.
14. Ibid., 243.
15. Ibid., 242.
16. Ricoeur, "The Critique of Religion," trans. R. Bradley DeFord, in *The Philosophy of Paul Ricoeur*, 213–22.
17. Paul Ricoeur, *The Conflict of Interpretations*, 148.
18. Ibid.
19. Erik H. Erikson, *Young Man Luther* (New York: W. W. Norton, 1958), 17.
20. Ibid., 220.

CHAPTER 2

1. Paul Ricoeur, "The Model of the Text," in *Social Research*.
2. Paul Ricoeur, "Metaphor and the Main Problem of Hermeneutics," in *Social Research*, 144.
3. Ricoeur, "The Model of the Text," in *Social Research*, 543.
4. This case is reported by Henri J. M. Nouwen in *Creative Ministry* (Garden City, N.Y.: Image Books, 1978), 43–45. It was used by permission from Seward Hiltner.
5. For a discussion of diagnosis as part of the dynamic process, not separate from it, see Donald Capps, *Pastoral Counseling and Preaching* (Philadelphia: Westminster Press, 1980), chap. 3.
6. Paul W. Pruyser, *The Minister as Diagnostician* (Philadelphia: Westminster Press, 1976), and William B. Oglesby, Jr., *Biblical Themes for Pastoral Care* (Nashville: Abingdon Press, 1980). I have correlated Pruyser's theological themes with Erik Erikson's psychological stages in Donald Capps, *Pastoral Care: A Thematic Approach* (Philadelphia: Westminster Press, 1979), chap. 4.
7. McFague, *Metaphorical Theology*, 55.
8. Erik H. Erikson, *Identity: Youth and Crisis* (New York: W. W. Norton, 1968), 220.
9. E. D. Hirsch, Jr., "Old and New in Hermeneutics," in *The Aims of Interpretation* (Chicago: University of Chicago Press, 1976), 17–35.
10. Ibid., 20.
11. Ibid., 25.
12. Ibid., 32.
13. Ibid.
14. Ibid.
15. See Wayne E. Oates, *Pastoral Care and Counseling in Grief and Separation* (Philadelphia: Fortress Press, 1976).

16. See Seward Hiltner, *Preface to Pastoral Theology* (Nashville: Abingdon Press, 1958), chap. 4. Paul W. Pruyser also argues for a perspectival approach in *The Minister as Diagnostician*, chap. 1.
17. See Erik H. Erikson, *Toys and Reasons* (New York: W. W. Norton, 1977). Erik Erikson's theory of ritualization may serve as an important bridge between psychological and sociological analyses of pastoral actions. See my *Life Cycle Theory and Pastoral Care* (Philadelphia: Fortress Press, 1983), chap. 3.
18. See Campbell, *Rediscovering Pastoral Care*, 26.
19. Ibid., chaps. 3–5.

CHAPTER 3
1. James E. Dittes, *The Minister on the Spot* (New York: Pilgrim Press, 1970), 102–27.
2. Capps, *Biblical Approaches to Pastoral Counseling*, chap. 3.
3. Capps, *Pastoral Care: A Thematic Approach*, chap. 2.
4. Capps, *Pastoral Counseling and Preaching*, chap. 4.
5. Langdon B. Gilkey, "The Roles of the 'Descriptive' or 'Historical' and of the 'Normative' in Our Work," *Criterion* 20 (1981): 10–17.
6. Newman S. Cryer and John M. Vayhinger, eds., *Casebook in Pastoral Counseling* (Nashville: Abingdon Press, 1962), 117–20.
7. See Campbell, *Rediscovering Pastoral Care*, 41.
8. Seward Hiltner, *Pastoral Counseling* (Nashville: Abingdon Press, 1949), 21–22.
9. Campbell, *Rediscovering Pastoral Care*, 47.
10. Ibid.
11. Ibid., 50.
12. Ibid., 51.
13. Henri J. M. Nouwen, *The Wounded Healer* (Garden City, N.Y.: Doubleday & Co., 1972), 94.
14. Heije Faber, *Pastoral Care in the Modern Hospital* (Philadelphia: Westminster Press, 1972). See also my discussion of this image in Donald Capps, *Life Cycle Theory and Pastoral Care* (Philadelphia: Fortress Press, 1983), chap. 5.
15. Campbell, *Rediscovering Pastoral Care*, 65.

CHAPTER 4
1. On the disclosive effects of such jolting of expectations, see James E. Dittes, *When the People Say No* (San Francisco: Harper & Row, 1979), chap. 5.

CHAPTER 5
1. Paul Ricoeur, *The Symbolism of Evil*, trans. Emerson Buchanan (Boston: Beacon Press, 1969) and *Time and Narrative*, vol. 1 (Chicago: University of Chicago Press, 1984).
2. Augustine, *The Confessions of St. Augustine*, trans. John K. Ryan (Garden City, N.Y.: Doubleday & Co., 1960).
3. Elie Wiesel, *Night*, trans. Stella Rodway (New York: Avon Books, 1969).

4. Donald Capps, "The Parabolic Event in Religious Autobiography," *Princeton Seminary Bulletin* 4 (1983): 26–38.

5. John Dominic Crossan, *The Dark Interval* (Niles, Ill.: Argus Communications, 1975), 57.

6. I have applied this model of the parable to pastoral care and counseling. See Capps, *Pastoral Counseling and Preaching*, 127–29, and *Biblical Approaches to Pastoral Counseling*, chap. 4.

7. See Norman Perrin, *Jesus and the Language of the Kingdom* (Philadelphia: Fortress Press, 1976), chap. 3.

8. Edmund Gosse, *Father and Son* (New York: Charles Scribner's Sons, 1916), 267–69.

9. For another example of a pastoral action to which this parable is relevant, see Capps, *Pastoral Care: A Thematic Approach*, 146–56.

10. Walter Breuggemann, *In Man We Trust* (Richmond: John Knox Press, 1972), 110–11.

11. T. S. Eliot, *Collected Poems 1909–1935* (New York: Harcourt, Brace, 1936).

12. James Olney drew attention to this feature of autobiography in *Metaphors of Self* (Princeton: Princeton University Press, 1972). The role of metaphor in pastoral action is also receiving increasing attention. See my discussion of metaphor in pastoral counseling in Capps, *Biblical Approaches to Pastoral Counseling*, 206–8. Also David S. Pacini, "Professionalism, Breakdown, and Revelation," in *Building Effective Ministry*, ed. Carl S. Dudley (San Francisco: Harper & Row, 1983), 133–52.

13. William L. Howarth, "Some Principles of Autobiography," in *Autobiography: Essays Theoretical and Critical*, ed. James Olney (Princeton: Princeton University Press, 1980), 84–114.

14. Dorothy Day, *The Long Loneliness* (San Francisco: Harper & Row, 1952).

15. On this point, see Elizabeth W. Bruss, *Autobiographical Acts: The Changing Situation of a Literary Genre* (Baltimore: Johns Hopkins University Press, 1976), 38.

16. H. Richard Niebuhr, *The Responsible Self*. Much current discussion of human development from a Christian ethical standpoint centers on the responsible self. See James W. Fowler, *Stages of Faith* (San Francisco: Harper & Row, 1981); J. Eugene Wright, Jr., *Erikson: Identity and Religion* (New York: Seabury Press, 1982); Carol Gilligan, "Justice and Responsibility: Thinking About Real Dilemmas of Moral Conflict and Choice," in *Toward Moral and Religious Maturity*, ed. Christiane Brusselmans (Morristown, N.J.: Silver Burdett, 1980), 224–49.

17. C. S. Lewis, *Surprised by Joy* (New York: Harcourt Brace Jovanovich, 1955).

18. Erving Goffman, *Behavior in Public Places* (New York: Free Press, 1963), 151–90.

19. Henri J. M. Nouwen, *Creative Ministry*, 38.

20. For a personal account of just this transformation, see Lewis R. Rambo, *The Divorcing Christian* (Nashville: Abingdon Press, 1983).

21. Crossan, *The Dark Interval*, 55.

22. Peterson, *Five Smooth Stones for Pastoral Work* (Atlanta: John Knox Press, 1980); Oglesby, *Biblical Themes for Pastoral Care;* Capps, *Biblical Approaches to Pastoral Counseling.*

23. See Paul S. Minear, *Images of the Church in the New Testament* (Philadelphia: Westminster Press, 1960).